VOW

A MEMOIR OF MARRIAGE (AND OTHER AFFAIRS)

WENDY PLUMP

BLOOMSBURY

LONDON · NEW DELHI · NEW YORK · SYDNEY

First published in Great Britain 2013

Copyright © 2013 by Wendy Plump

The moral right of the author has been asserted

No part of this book may be used or reproduced in any manner whatsoever without
written permission from the Publisher except in the case of brief quotations embodied in
critical articles or reviews

Bloomsbury Publishing Plc
50 Bedford Square
London
WC1B 3DP

www.bloomsbury.com

Bloomsbury Publishing, London, New Delhi, New York and Sydney
A CIP catalogue record for this book is available from the British Library

ISBN 978 1 4088 2780 2
10 9 8 7 6 5 4 3 2 1

Designed by Sara Stemen
Typeset by Westchester Book Group
Printed and bound by CPI Group (UK) Ltd, Croydon, CR0 4YY

MIX
Paper from
responsible sources
FSC® C020471

FOR THE HENS

Hunger allows no choice . . .

—W. H. AUDEN, "SEPTEMBER 1, 1939"

CONTENTS

CONTENTS

FINDING OUT

FROM A FRIEND. From the cell phone. From a neighbor. From e-mails left on the computer. From hotel receipts. From a homemade sex video tragically left out in the open. From the bank account. From the dog sitter. From the nanny. Especially if it is the nanny. From the spouse. From the lover. From an offhand comment on the playground. From the monthly expenses that don't jibe with anything you did or received or gave. From the cashier at the lumberyard. From some weird supermarket encounter. From your mother, whose antennae have been tuned to this frequency much longer than you realize. From the accumulation of doubt. From walking in on them in the office. From walking in on them in the bedroom. From walking in on them.

So many ways to find out. So many ways.

Four months before I found out my husband was having an affair, a school in the North Caucasus in Russia was stormed by Chechnyan separatists, and over three days eleven hundred hostages were taken, including eight hundred schoolchildren. It ended badly—even, I imagine, for those who got away with their lives.

The Beslan hostage crisis still pierces my awareness many years later because of the small, stubborn role it played in the unveiling of my husband's last affair. The events were unrelated and on two different sides of the world, but they are conjoined in my memory of them. Details fall into the crevices between life-altering knowledge and your reaction to it. These details take on their own significance by filling up the space between, adding buffer and firewall and salt indeed to the whole mess of finding out.

A friend came over one morning in early January 2005 because she thought it was time to tell me about Bill. My two sons were at elementary school. It had been snowing hard for two days, almost canceling school and a party the previous weekend during which our friends hotly debated the merits of marriage. I recall announcing to the dinner table with stupid conviction, "Even if I thought it was the best idea, I would never get a divorce." I have always been a fool in the court of conspicuous declaration. I remember once telling someone in eighth grade that I would never smoke pot, never have sex before marriage, never sneak out of my bedroom window in pursuit of a guy. I was a holy horror of sanctimony. Within five years I had done all of those things.

I wish I had had my wits about me more back then, and now. Things happened that I was oblivious to even as they were happening to me or because of me, including the folly of my own behavior. I knew nothing solid about myself as a young woman, right up to and possibly including yesterday.

When my friend came through the front door that morning in January—letting herself in without knocking because that is how we operate—I came out of my bedroom and looked down at her from the top of the staircase. She was agitated, out of sorts, as if she were holding herself upright against a heavy blast of wind. This was not hindsight. It was an instant telegraphing of something critical, something disturbing. Are you okay? was my first question. And her reply, pressed into my very veins: It's not me. It's you.

2

Here's where the Chechnyans came into it. I thought she was there to tell me that my sons' elementary school had been stormed by insurgents. This was partly ridiculous and partly terror, the wild but typical response of an overanxious parent. You are always in reconnaissance mode once your babies are on the ground. My oldest son was born one month after Timothy McVeigh blew up the federal building in Oklahoma City. That horror and its attendant crowd of loss jump-started my mother-fear. The worst of the world's events are seared into my psyche more so than before I was a parent because tragedy echoes through my concern for my sons. That January morning, it took my friend several minutes to calm me down by repeating over and over, It's not the boys. It's not the boys. It's not the boys.

Until finally, and no doubt partly out of exasperation, she blurted out: It's Bill. He's having an affair.

This news fell into place with an almost audible click. Like a bullet revolving in its cylinder and lining up with the chamber. The violent image fits because it was a kind of violence that I lived with later on. But right then, right in that moment, what I most remember thinking is, This makes sense. It wasn't shock. It was relief that I felt. There were no Chechnyans at my sons' elementary school, where seconds before I had visualized them storming art class. That was not the case. What else was there to worry about?

There had been so many holes in our marriage over the preceding years. Late night movies that Bill attended apparently on his own. Claims that he had been driving around smoking a cigar—"Just thinking"—until late into the night. Evenings when I would find him alone outside, staring into the fields behind our house. I felt such a deep disconnect from him, a hum of disturbance not far

3

below the surface of domestic routine. When I heard the news of his affair, the disconnect was blown away. The news explained a lot. Everything, really.

People are incredulous when I say that I did not suspect anything before this discovery. They think I must have been aware that Bill was having an affair, as if suspicion were linked to some primal instinct we all have. I have no idea what imperative suspicion would serve Neanderthals such that it would repeat upward through the species to find its expression in us. Would it make you more accomplished in sacking cavepeople? It seems unlikely that Java Man had the neural complexity to doubt. Doubt is a scourge of incipient sophistication. Life would be pleasanter without it.

In any case, this was not even remotely true. Despite a history of affairs on both our sides by that late point—my own affairs were earlier in the marriage, and Bill's affairs were later—it hadn't occurred to me that Bill was fooling around. One time I looked for his movie ticket stubs and duly found them. Once I wondered why he never let me borrow his cell phone. Once I asked him where he had been until two A.M. the night before. I always got answers that did not exactly satisfy, but that worked.

They worked because the explanations you most want to hear are also the easiest to deliver. They require so little evidence. One sentence will suffice, something short and offered up by your spouse with a surfeit of confidence. After which you can go on with the laundry or the homework or the purchase of cleaning products. There is a lot to do in a family.

The acceptance of a lame alibi is part of the larger web of complicity I share with my husband. I am aware of not having suspected. But I am also aware that I would not have wanted to suspect. At its

4

worst, suspicion will eat you alive. At its least, it is a bore. It interferes with life itself. Each time I felt the edge of suspicion crowding me, I would ask, and he would answer. And I would exhale and take the answer in hand and go about my day. I did not suspect any more than that because that would have been inconvenient to all the things I wanted to do. Continuing my marriage being one of them.

So, again. When my friend said Bill was having an affair, everything made immediate sense. I did not doubt it. I knew I would feel like hell later on. But right at that moment, clarity, even of something terrible, was an odd but certain kind of rest.

The news did in fact go downhill from there.

At what point in my life did the concept of Finding Out take a continual turn for the worse? It used to be that Finding Out was a kind of gift. It's how you grew up, learned, started to pick your way along the more ragged edges of your experiences. When I was younger, I found out all manner of useful and happy things. I found out that my parents loved me. That my grandfather was a masterful storyteller. That dogs spun around three times before lying down.

I found out that the little box my parents brought home from New York City when I was ten held a kitten. That horses could in fact drink from a hose. That I could boss my little sister around, but just until she grew taller than me. That you could in fact sit in a tree during a thunderstorm and not get struck by lightning.

I found out there was fun to be had with the opposite sex in basements and in laundry rooms. That sex was strange and astonishingly good. That men actually do want to make you happy. I found out that Bill wanted to marry me. That honeymoons were precious. And that no matter how incompetent I felt as a mother, my infant sons preferred me to all others.

5

Somewhere along the way, though, Finding Out became a massive drag. Maybe this is what it is to be an adult, moving along the arc of your life's luck and misfortune and accumulating its downers. Now we Find Out about cancer, about infidelity, about a child's sickness, about a school shooting, about a neighbor diagnosed with leukemia, about an insurrection that leads to a war that leads to young soldiers dying. These were present when we were younger, but not so searingly. They were not about us. They happened in Scotland or Da Nang or Wisconsin. But as we age, the odds increase that we are standing on ground zero.

I imagine Bill would say the same thing, for he experienced shock and betrayal at my hands, too. How did he Find Out about me for the first time? I told him.

I had three affairs before I had children, early in my marriage — with Tommy, who came into my life through a girlfriend; then with Steven, whom I met on a marina dock in South Carolina; then with Terry, a local hunter who taught me how to practice archery. Each affair knocked into the next, like dominoes, and for a little while took down everything and everyone in the vicinity. Bill was anguished over the discoveries of them. And since they came one on the heels of another, I'm not sure how he slogged through it. He did not ever wish to discuss anything with me in great detail. He recovered without the trickle of dialogue. But he recovered. He stayed in the marriage, is my point.

In time, however, Bill would trump that history. He betrayed me with several women. But while those earlier discoveries were hard to bear, they weren't devastating to our marriage. Each time I found out about him, I wanted our marriage to survive and continue. I learned after each one to live with the realities of his affairs and then just went on. I would not have ended it under the earlier circumstances.

Finally, though, Bill had one of those affairs that shock the whole pond and change all the life forms in it. So that nothing could thrive there afterward. I know this to be true because we had experienced so many scenarios of adultery already. We were a full-horizon couple. We had a 360-degree view of infidelity. We knew it from every angle.

Now that I look back, I can see how much of my life's energy has gone toward infidelity, from both Bill's side and from my own, almost as if I were on a mission. To give in to it, to get past it, to understand it, to force its influence from our marriage. I am dismayed that this is one of the guiding patterns of my life. In the way that the ancient Silk Road is marked out across the planet from space—though you cannot see it from the ground—adultery has carved its own passage through my life, made most visible these days through perspective and distance. It looks like a blast corridor.

Mine is not a strict cautionary tale. It is one tale. Or one version of a tale. There are more versions, more stories, of infidelity out there than there are married people, since you tell the same story many times and change it according to mood and audience, editing for effect, both magnifying and playing down the details. It also reflects the experiences of just two adults, and one of them more than the other. It is a very specific story. I am not an expert in the subject apart from what happened with us. There are millions of different unions, and they all have their own DNA. This is ours, the story of our marriage and all the hopeful and misguided behaviors we brought to it. So while it reflects just one couple's union, it enters the stream of all marriages, weighting the whole institution with its lessons.

7

I can lay claim to this general truth, though: Of all the things there are to do on the planet, my husband and I picked one hell of a pastime. If we had it to do over again, I imagine the very same things would happen once more. Had we been able to change ourselves early enough to make a lasting difference, we probably would have done that already.

Bill and I met in college when we were nineteen and were married eight years later. We were barely a year into our marriage and had just moved into our first home in Pennsylvania when I met Tommy. I was ignorant when I married Bill. I assumed the gravity and laws of marriage—not to mention the love I felt for my husband—would be enough to prevent me from desiring anyone else. I was wrong about this.

By that point I had been in love twice: once with Tim, my boyfriend from high school, whose sweet relationship I carried with me into my freshman year at college; and then with Bill, who would become my husband in 1987. In love, I desired no one else. All the attraction, all the compulsion, all the hope for the future, went to one man. These seemed an effective demilitarized zone against temptation, and they are. They keep the enemies of the marriage at bay. But they weaken over the years without any siren going off to alert you to that fact. Their half-life ticks past silently. So I was thrown off balance when I first met Tommy and felt an attraction so compelling I no longer cared that I was married.

Like everything else, infidelity has its own learning curve. If you want, you can become proficient. You can stake out the signs of your vulnerability and indulge or ignore them depending on your moral position. But this was early in my marriage. No one close to me had experienced anything like it yet. There was no trusted ally to go to and ask, "What the hell is this feeling and why do I have it?" There was no playbook for temptation and its sudden, indisputable appearance in my life.

Tommy was the beautiful twin brother of my friend Sarah's fiancé. Sarah's brother-in-law-to-be. We met at a pub in Brandywine, Pennsylvania, amid a crush of people gathered to celebrate the couple. I recall meeting Sarah's fiancé and thinking, Oh my, an Errol Flynn look-alike; Sarah's done well for herself. Then I met his twin brother and thought, Oh my, another Errol Flynn look-alike. And this one I can in fact have. Tommy had a wicked white smile that flashed a message. It said, I want to take you home. It said, Forget your husband and come with me. It said, Of all the people in this town, I want you. I abandoned myself to the scene and to the man. We ended up later that night in some grassy field, drunk on vodka and crazy to get at each other.

Bill was traveling constantly in those days. Russia, China, London, meant weeks of being alone and unmonitored. For both of us. In the days before the ubiquity of cell phone use, not being reachable was a fair excuse. I was at Tommy's apartment often. I was not reachable. I should have been concentrating on our new house, our new jobs, our new dog, Rogue, who kept biting the neighbors. The early days of domesticity should have a wide-eyed sweetness—where should we put the butter dish, how many pillows do you sleep with, why do you have six sticks of deodorant—but all of it was compromised by my affair. The first years of our marriage carried a blight, and I had smuggled it in.

A few months into it, the stress of the affair with Tommy actually started to hurt physically. I felt as though I had dysentery. At home I was anxious and ill at ease. At Tommy's apartment I was passionate but distracted. At work I was bitchy and unfocused. The fear that I would be found out was all-consuming. I wanted to put an end to it.

I don't know that Bill was noticing the same gaps I would notice years later, those absences created around adultery when you are not where you say you are. His endless travel made both of our deceptions easier, but you can't always have an alibi or your life starts sounding like someone's billable hours: "I was at work and then I went out for coffee with a whole bunch of people and then I stopped at the gas station and then I bought dog food and then I stopped to buy you your favorite brand of cookies. Oreos. Double. You believe me, right?" Sound overly earnest and you will draw the wolves of suspicion out of the woods.

Lies are easy to forget, too. Or, put another way, it's easy to forget what you made up in the thick of the moment to cover your absence. After a few days you can't recall if you said you were out with Jean or out with Jean and Babs, or out with Sarah and her fiancé or if you were just at the movies by yourself. Or with Jean and Sarah at the movies. Or with your sister. Or what movie you had seen. Or you were supposed to meet someone who bailed so you never actually saw the movie. You were driving around smoking a cigar—"Just thinking"—until late into the night.

It becomes too much to keep track of unless you plan on scribbling everything down in your infidelity ledger. I would build just enough truth into my excuses that they would be easier for me to remember. I would say where I had been but not precisely whom I had been with. Or I would use the phrase "a whole bunch of people." This Bill came to hate. It was a red flag for him even before he knew why. This is easy to understand. Any spouse who is even half-awake would prick up his ears at such defiant nonspecificity.

One night I came home from that bar in Brandywine where I had been with Tommy and a whole bunch of people. It was three A.M. This was Pennsylvania, not Rio. Nothing was open that late. So being out until that hour was a blazing flare shot into the night sky, illuminating the situation vividly.

I walked slowly up into the darkness of our second-floor home, the air growing warmer and stiller. Everything was asleep, all in its place. Apart from me. I walked into my bedroom, where Bill was sleeping, and found our dog, Rogue, stretched out across the bed next to him. In my place. Where I slept. The dog was never allowed up on our bed. He had never been there before. I wondered at his presence. I wondered if Bill had invited him up there against the suspicion he felt, as comfort and as company. Rogue did not move when he saw me. Dogs are keen as hell. So heavy was my guilt that I believed he sensed my betrayal and wasn't about to budge for some adulteress. I believed he was punishing me in his own canine way. At that point I realized I had had enough. Rather than continue to observe the slow unhinging of my mind and the ascribing of judgment to the family pet, I decided to stop the affair.

There is a centripetal force to every affair. Once it starts, once it gets cranking in its whirl of lies and pleasure, it is a bitch to slow down. And to disembark without getting knocked over, forget it. I did not think I would be able to do that on my own. Breaking off from Tommy had become essential but I did not know how to do it. I didn't want to continue the deceit, but I also didn't want to give him up. It was the drug of him that I wanted: the sex, the feel of a new body, the way he looked me over as if he had never seen a woman before. It would be next to impossible for me to resist this infatuation on my own. Quitting him, I came to realize, would require a massive opposing force. Something like the truth would do.

This counsel came from an old high school friend. Kate and I had spent so much time talking, laughing, crying, and analyzing everything in our path as young women that there was nothing we didn't know each about the other. She lived behind me across a wild, unmown field where we smoked early cigarettes and hid from her brother. We came of age full of the drama of young women at the mercy of first loves and parents, formidable forces both. Sometimes she came knocking on my ground-floor window in the middle of the night, distraught after being mistreated once again by her father. (It was true—he was awful.) So I believed Kate when she told me, This is how to stop your affair. Tell Bill. Tell him. That is how he should Find Out. Something in the way she said it made me believe I could make an ally out of Bill.

There is no way to do this well. It is the grim task faced by doctors who have to communicate a malignancy, police officers with bad news about a car crash, stockbrokers who must tell you that the deal went bust and all the money is gone. My resolve kicked in only because I knew that, for now, anything I felt should take a backseat to Bill's reaction. Including cowardice. I would deliver this short, noxious blast of information, and then I would step back to see what the immediate toll was and what was required of me next. That was my plan.

Bill walked into the house after work. It was winter by this point and dark outside by the time he got home. I was waiting for him, leaning against the narrow entryway. This in itself was unusual. I was not a door greeter. Bill said hello, walked past me, put his briefcase down, threw his jacket on the chair, and then looked back at me to ask what was up. We were not a kiss-hello sort of couple, either, although we always kissed good-bye.

I asked him to sit down. Please. But first I had to tell Rogue to get off the couch. He had crawled up there, an opportunist of the guilt in that household. "Rogue, get down!" I told him. Such a simple set of words belonging to an innocent domestic life that wouldn't exist in a matter of minutes. Oh, I longed for that life already.

Bill sat, his face turned up to mine, looking directly into my eyes, heart-stoppingly clueless. How many times had I looked into his face since we met and seen every expression there? Love, sadness, fury, euphoria, kindness, desire, confusion, happiness, drunkenness, contentment—sexual and otherwise. His face was wiped clean of all this. It had only a look of such absolute concentration and innocence as to unnerve me completely. If he had any idea what I was about to unload on him, he did not show it.

I had six words to speak. Six small words. Six life-altering words. It could just as easily have been six words about loving him or being pregnant with our first child or backing into the oak tree at the end of our driveway again. It was not. It was a whole new phylum of news. I paused in that space between knowledge and reaction. Buffer. Firewall. Salt. It is a very intimate space.

Bill, I am having an affair.

I wish I could say it took a minute for this to sink in. It did not. Bill's reaction was instantaneous, as if I had scattered acid on him. He snapped up from the couch, his face instantly pale, his mouth open, fury pouring from him. "Who?" he screamed.

I started to tell him. I said, "Sarah's fiancé's brother—," and that was all I got out. I had been spending a lot of time with these people. Bill knew that. He may have suspected already.

His reaction was explosive. He looked at me as if he hated me. He looked at me as if he had always hated me. He looked at me as if hatred were the only thing he would ever feel for me again. He was screaming, but I don't remember anything else he said. It was loud and it was violent and it drained the room of oxygen. He looked around wildly as if for something to smash. He bolted upstairs. Doors were slammed, and once he was inside our bedroom there was more crashing. He was locked in, and I wasn't given entry.

I hate thinking about this now. I hate my betrayal, but I also hate his fury. It doesn't matter if it makes sense or if you have no right to feel it. Their rage fills you up with your own rage. Mixed with shame and guilt, it is a wretched cocktail to swallow. It is horrible to hurt your spouse, and it is horrible to feel his rage at you. As though you are a bad child. As though you're the worst child in the world. It runs through you and connects you to every instance when you were bad and were found out, clear back to childhood. It is a very distinct feeling of shame. I wanted to spit the feeling out. I wanted to bash walls.

I did not see Bill until the next morning. I knocked on the bedroom door that night but was told to go away. I was desperate to talk to him, to soothe him, to tell him my affair need not mean our marriage was over. That it was him I loved. All of this would have been useless and also, I think now, unfair. It was Bill's turn to decide the moment. My part was to exist in a kind of mannered, patient stasis until he had something to say. I spent the night downstairs and slept on the couch, the dog just a few feet away.

When I came home from work the following night, Bill was

already there, upstairs in our bedroom. It was unlocked. I went in. He was lying on the bed, his arms thrown up over his face so that I could see only his mouth, a straight, grim line. I stood there beside him, looking down at the mess of him, and thought, I did that. That was me.

I do not question now my decision to tell him, to come clean. I didn't see that the marriage could continue with the weight of that secret between us. It was a whole second life that I was leading— affection, sex, experience, the knowledge of another human being, the nights spent with a man I wasn't married to. How do you absorb this into the whole of your life when that life is shared so intimately with a spouse? It's the deceit that causes the anguish. Not just for them. But for you. And when you finally want to end the thing, you want to end all of it. Including the burden of hiding it.

Finding Out is a demarcation, a line between before and after. It annihilates one and defines the other. When Finding Out involves something huge and life-changing, your acceptance of it is oddly instantaneous. You know. You didn't know a second before, but now you do. The disbelief, the struggle with acceptance, the inability to process, all come later. It's a reverse reaction, in my view. You know right away and you feel it right away. And then, sometime later, after you already believe it, *that's* when you have trouble believing it.

It must have something to do with unwillingness. You start to see how lousy this is going to be and you beat your hands against it. You rebel. I picture a child shaking his head vehemently in a tantrum of refusal. No, no, no. No. Don't want to Find Out. Don't want to know. Don't want to hear.

In this state you are convinced that the more you insist on No, the more likely you are to exert some influence in that direction. You will not, in the end, un-know this. But that makes little difference to your effort. Can I stop time? Can I back things up? Can I fly around the planet and reverse its course? It does not matter if this is irrational. It is how you think. You literally cast about for ways to accomplish this. You waste actual time on this. And you will do it whether you are hearing a confession or speaking one.

I wonder what would have been an easier way to Find Out, for either of us. The varieties of finding out are arrayed like the rungs of a ladder, such that hearing a rumor about the affair is on the bottom rung while finding your spouse in bed with a lover is at the top. Still, I don't know that it makes all that much of a difference to the suffering. And eventually, it doesn't make any difference. It all sucks. It all sucks so badly that after the initial Finding Out, the details of the discovery are just bad embroidery on the knowledge itself.

Adultery is a big-engine issue, one of the biggest confronting a marriage. Even if you are one of the lucky ones, rapturously happy in your choice and unmarked by deceit, it is still a confrontation for many people, an in-your-face question that haunts the peripheries of the union. Because while it may not ensnare every marriage, it will almost certainly ensnare some of those in the vicinity. Like all major confrontations, adultery seems simple from a distance. It presents as a single-celled organism—Don't!—and then evolves into a more complex creature over time and the more you look at it: What are the reasons for cheating? How do you resist? Why should you? Why shouldn't you? Where did our passion go? Who is that guy at the coffee counter with the gray eyes and the tool belt?

When I was newly married, I didn't know all that many people who had taken up the banner of temptation the way we had. A full

16

generation later, I know many. I wonder how accurately this reflects the phenomenon outside my own circle of friends and acquaintances. How many have cheated. How many are tempted. And most immediately, how many of them—married men and women, lesbians, college students, septuagenarians, people living on estates, people living on welfare, captains of industry, captains of the police department, PTO mothers, toy store employees, Realtors, toll takers, lawyers—are right now hearing that they have been betrayed. It could at any time be millions and millions. There should be a hotline for these beaten souls. There should be someone at the end of a phone somewhere who can respond to the Fury you become.

The Fury you become. When I was a young girl we had horses, but one in particular I loved more than the others. This horse, a Thoroughbred recently bought off of the racetrack, was an undeniable wing nut. She had a fancy registered name, but I just called her Mare. That would be on a par with someone just calling me Vessel. But anyway.

Mare was so tightly wound that the smallest thing would freak her out. I'd have her clipped into the cross-ties at the barn for a good grooming. A currying down, liniment oil on her legs, hooves picked. But occasionally something would set her off. I'd pick up a soft brush and *wham*! She'd flip out. She'd sit way back on her haunches as far as the cross-ties would stretch, eyes thrown wide and white, nostrils flaring. And you could hear the wooden beams to which she was slotted beginning to creak under the strain. I often feared she would pull the whole barn down.

The only thing that helped was a steady hand following the long curve of her shoulder and a soft voice saying, "Easy, Mare. Easy." Time and time again. Downward sweep of my hand. Calm

17

voice intoning. After a minute or two, her eyes would blink and her nostrils would flare down. She'd settle slowly forward and the cross-ties would ease again and hang loose. I'd pat her gently a few more times and then pick up the very brush that had set her off. And everything would be fine.

This is what I think about when I hear that someone has just Found Out. They are animal wild in their grief, braced back on their haunches, the cross-ties—meaning anything that binds them to the sentient world—straining as if to snap. They need a steadying hand. A gentle voice. No vitriol. No hysterics. No words other than "Easy, love. Easy." Sometimes you have to go to animal ground to get yourself back again.

I didn't have access to Bill's thoughts on the matter after he found out about Tommy or any of the others. He never wanted to talk about my affairs or his own. But I remember one particular night we spent on vacation, months after he found out about Tommy, who, it must be said, disappeared almost without a trace after my confession.

Bill and I had gone away to restore ourselves back to ourselves. We were young and everything seemed elastic and recoverable, even our marriage. The vacation was my idea, an attempt to do something. I needed to shape a solution out of thin air. After all, what are the building blocks for this kind of repair? Trust? Gone. Reflection? Thinking straight is the last thing you can do. Advice? At such a time, few can give it dispassionately. So. Vacation and time together, desperate and clichéd, were the tools I came up with.

I had bought lingerie for the trip to reclaim our sex life. I hoped it would come across as pretty, fetching. I wanted to be alluring but sort of sweet. Fishnet stockings, for example, were out. I wanted innocence back again and was just delusional enough to think that might be possible. Big mistake. If anyone does that well, it is not the woman who has just cuckolded her husband.

There I stood in our hotel room, the Caribbean Sea as backdrop, in my satin and high-cut lace. And Bill took one look at me and caved into gloom. He turned away and lay down on the bed. He wouldn't talk to me anymore that night. He went to sleep, and I knew why. I could see on his face what he was thinking. I wasn't only his wife. I was someone who had worn lingerie for someone else, and recently, and after I said I would forsake all others. And again a small part of my self stood back from him and watched his sorrow, thinking, I did this. I am bad.

Sometimes you can control the Finding Out. You can either confess or you can wait through your spouse's suspicion until it's discovered. If you are on the other side of it, you can force a confrontation or you can wait to have your suspicions confirmed. Both constitute a form of ownership and a choice to be made.

Early in our marriage, I chose to tell Bill when I was having an affair partly because I couldn't stand the stress of him not knowing. You cannot have a life with someone when half of that life is sealed off behind a wall of lies. Over the years, Bill chose to wait it out when he was having an affair, I assume because he just did not want to be the one to tell me. I don't see that it makes that much difference in the end. You've already given up the moral high ground once you start screwing around.

But there is the smallest amount of control you can assert. It's all you will have for a very long time. You have to use it well, and the only opportunity to do so is up front. It is after the Finding Out that control starts to drift sidewise and on a current not of your own making. You have to prepare yourself for that, knowing that once those words leave your mouth or once someone finds out, there will be no predicting the next few hours, the next few weeks, the next few months. By virtue of the confession, you are turning your spouse into someone you do not know. You cannot count on his or her reaction. You have no indication of how your spouse will feel under this circumstance.

There is nothing else like infidelity. The very novelty of it in the relationship means you have likely not faced this situation before, and there are no signposts on this road apart from the road itself to tell you what's ahead. You think your spouse is composed in the presence of trauma? This is a whole new world of trauma. You think your spouse is incapable of violence? Infidelity hurts so much that she will want to break the chair, smash the television, claw at her own face. You are married to a screamer? The shock of this news could bring on a dead calm that will be worse than any screaming.

Any attempt on your part to control it will muck it up even more. You have no right to control, because what you have been doing with your responsibility for the last several months nullifies your claim. You betrayed your spouse. Say your piece, sit down, be quiet. That was the only response I figured my revelation would allow me. That was the only way I could imagine getting through the Finding Out part. That is what I did. As soon as I told Bill about my affair, I could no longer manage the tilt of our marriage. It drifted out of my control, its tides caught up and dictated by Bill's grief.

And when I found out about Bill's final affair, I no longer had a say in my own conduct for a very long time.

I lost that command right about the time my girlfriend showed up that January morning in 2005 and told me the rest of the news she had come to reveal. Once she had said that Bill was having an affair, she added a few more things.

Wendy, she told me, Bill has a house with another woman about a mile away from your house. And it is the same woman he had an affair with several years ago. And they have a child. A son. Who is now eight months old.

I am fairly sure—though I blinked out of real consciousness for several days—I am fairly sure that once I heard that last fragment, I pulled the whole barn down.

COMBAT STRESS

S HE LIVES HERE," my sister told me of Bill's mistress, handing me a slip of paper with her address written on it the
night we found out she existed. "Do you want me to go over
there with you?" Do I want you to go over there with me?
This was not a question as I heard it. It was a series of words thrown
out into the airless room where we were standing. A series of words.
Whatever they are. I played with them in my head, batting them
around absently while my patient sister awaited an answer.

For the first soul-shocked hours of knowing about Bill's mistress and baby, this is how I processed words and images: piecemeal
and very slowly, as if I'd suffered a head trauma. I moved at a glacial
pace. I pawed through every utterance as if looking for clues. Reality was so out of kilter that even the structure of a simple question
had to be driven through a code breaker in my head as a way to
make sense of it. Nothing could be taken at face value. The whole
house seemed made of vapor. Nothing was reliable. Home was not
safe. Family was not inviolate. Husband was not mine. Sky was not
blue. I looked at the small piece of paper in my hands that listed her
address. Her house was only about a mile from ours. Not surprising.
Most shark attacks occur in just a few feet of water.

It was late. I had had a house full of people for most of that day,
all arriving from various points when they heard the news. I wasn't

the only one with processing difficulties. Everyone was trying to make sense of the discovery. My parents were flying home stunned and early from their vacation in South Carolina. My brother and sister shook their heads silently at each other and offered to spend the night with me. Friends were milling about, pouring tea and vodka in equal measure. I was clearly out of it. I think everyone was afraid I might accidentally leave the gas stove on or commit a felony or forget where the bedrooms were. I was in shock. I don't mean surprise. I mean the literal, grasping fog of shock. I could not even discern that I had been wronged. Bill has a girlfriend? And they have a house? And they have a baby who is eight months old? What does that even mean?

I wanted to call Bill at work. He was in Mississippi for the week, as the company he worked for had a subsidiary office there. I remember walking toward the phone at the far end of the kitchen when the friend who had given me the news earlier that day stepped in front of me. "Are you sure you want to do this?" she asked. "Are you ready to talk with him?" Yes, I was. I needed this disaster confirmed. That my friends had given ample evidence was indisputable. Still, some little voice at the back of my mind held out for a mistake. I knew what I would hear when I spoke to Bill. But I hoped for something else. I don't remember exactly what I said to him when I got him on the phone. Only that he answered with two words: "It's true." It's true. Whatever you just said is true. That thing about a girlfriend and a baby is true. And the baby is eight months old. Yes. It's true. I think I spent the rest of the afternoon circling the couch like a wounded bird.

Truth was a concept Bill and I had distorted so utterly over the years that it was impossible to grasp the simplicity of it then. I had to focus on it very carefully. I had to think about what was true in that moment and only in that moment. By that point it was true that my friends and brother had just left. That my sons—just five and eight at the time—were finally in bed. That it was snowing. That it was nighttime. That I had to make a decision about going somewhere. My sister was standing in front of me with an address. The address was there, too, in my hands. Did I want to go over, and did I want her to go with me?

I had already been told at least twenty times since that morning that I should not do this or there was the possibility that I could lose my children. I should not confront Her or do anything remotely threatening or I could lose my children. I should not attempt to enter her house or approach her or I could lose my children. The specter of losing my children loomed over every move I might have made, and it scared me into submission.

Of course, this wasn't a serious possibility. I came to realize eventually that even if I was adjudged by a flock of mullahs, it was unlikely that I would lose my children owing to my husband's adultery. Still, my sister's question revealed the deepest form of devotion. She knew that going over to the mistress's house could have been a disaster and possibly illegal. Well, she's an attorney. She thinks a clear path. But she had been willing to do that regardless of the consequence on the small chance that it would help me make sense of my new reality. That was actually the second thing she had handed me that day. The first was a bar of chocolate. She arrived earlier, holding just that one thing—a Toblerone bar—and she gave it to me as soon as I opened the door. She held it out to me anxiously and clearly at a loss. As if she wanted to do some small thing that was ordinary and innocent and had nothing at all to do with finding out.

We eventually decided not to make the trip to the mistress's house. I couldn't imagine at that late point that there would be anything worth seeing, and certainly nothing that would answer my anguish. Anyway, I didn't want to go over. What I wanted to do was go up to my room and turn out the lights. Climb into bed. Have some silence around me. Try to parse one time through the full meaning of this sentence: Bill has a longtime girlfriend and a baby who is eight months old.

Later, in the dark, that is what I did: Bill—my husband of eighteen years; has a longtime girlfriend—just how long I would soon find out; and a baby, who is eight months old—he has been eight months upon this earth and I didn't know it?

My mind ran through the previous year. Where had we been eight months ago? The answer came quickly. My sons and I had been in South Carolina eight months ago. That had been our pattern every July for years, since the boys were born. If it was July, we were in South Carolina. It began to look almost as if everything had been planned and that I had been played brilliantly. This engendered a whole new round of shock. I don't even think I cried. I couldn't knock any meaning into that sentence after all. It bewildered me beyond comprehension.

The sensation of emotional shock feels like suspension. We are animals and we have been designed this way as part of an adaptive psychology. When you experience shock, your adrenal gland releases epinephrine, a kind of flash-flood hormone. It courses through the body, calling every system to attention so that your blood vessels constrict, your heart races, your muscles tighten, your breathing quickens—all the behaviors necessary for combat or escape. Fight or flight.

But later, fogginess ensues. You hang above your own reality, are pulled out of it by a protective stress response that doesn't want you exposed too quickly. So you look down on your world as if it's happening to someone else. In this way you take in the news a little bit at a time. This is the body's idea of a soft landing. Of course, it's only temporary. Shock wears off in a day or two and then you will have to deal in the way that a broken bone is most painful the day after the break. Still, here is biology at its finest. The work of some neuron firing through the disorder of your mind and streaming this banner behind it: I will cover you with a fog so that you can think, but not too clearly, while you adjust the frame of your perspective. So do that. Adjust. Soon.

When I was little I used to ride my bike around my neighborhood in Green Valley, Pennsylvania, with my eyes closed, which was inconvenient for the neighbors. It was a common enough skill, but one whose usefulness to adulthood I was not aware of then. It taught me how to move forward without relying on the usual markers. To trust in my animal balance. To ride blind. It is a talent you can access in dire need.

The morning after I was told about Bill's mistress and baby, I accessed it. I moved through my normal routine with my eyes shut. I rode blind. The skill came back to me so effortlessly that I stayed locked in that mode for most of 2005. It didn't blunt the sadness, but it did keep the household on a somewhat evener keel. The following morning, I had to make sandwiches and fill my sons' lunch boxes. I had to feed the dog. I was a reporter for a newspaper, so I had to write a story intelligibly. I had to go into my youngest son's kindergarten class and make ducks out of egg cartons. We had a life. Its responsibilities had to be honored regardless of who was living across town. I'm amazed at how much can be accomplished in an emotional coma.

Later that morning, I was standing over my son's little table of kindergarten students when a teacher who knew something of my situation appeared suddenly at the classroom door. As if someone had notified her. As if she'd gotten this message: "Wendy Plump is in the building. Please locate and appraise the situation."

I had known this woman for a long time. She had navigated some nasty marital issues of her own with astonishing grace and was admired for this by those who knew her. Apparently, she had known for many months beforehand about the situation with Bill and his mistress. Thinking on it now, I am aware of the small army of people who must have known what it took me so long to discover. The mistress's siblings (six of them), her parents, their friends, the tree guy, the man who did the ductwork, the paper delivery boy, the neighbor across the street. A veritable crowd of onlookers in various states of appall had a share in this intimate knowledge. This teacher had been one of them. She looked into the kindergarten classroom with an expression of deep kindness on her face. She knew I was held together with duct tape. She simply found my gaze and smiled at me warmly. Like a mother. Like a mother superior. A shot of strength ran through me, as if I had just been adrenalized.

Later, after the egg carton ducks, I drove over to the mistress's house. Just to see. It was in a neighborhood that I had known since high school. Friends had lived there years ago, and a few even remained. It felt weird to be back there under those circumstances. I had taken tennis lessons from a boy who had lived around the bend. My parents were friends with several older couples still living there. My school bus had rumbled through that neighborhood with me

on it. So here I was again. Well, it would never have any other reso-
nance for me from that point on.

A current of curiosity ran through me. I had to see her house. I
half expected it to be shrouded with a massive tarp, like a crime
scene, so good was Bill at covering things up. But no. There it was
in plain daylight, a two-story, stone-fronted home with a big lawn
and a big picture window. As I drew up and stopped the car in front
of the house, I saw someone standing before the window holding a
baby in her arms. Was that the other woman? No. Too old. Too fat.
What would Bill want with such a person? It was likely the mistress's
mother or an aunt standing there so the baby could look out upon
the world.

I stared, struggling to take in the visual while a mincing, ob-
noxious voice in my head hollered out obvious answers to my confusion. Is that a baby? *Of course it's a baby.* Is that Bill's child? *Of
course it's his child, who else would it be?* Who is that person holding
him? *What do you care, you hate her no matter who she is.* Why am
I in such a fog? *Because you've been had. Apparently you've been living in that fog for far too long.*

My mind floated back through the possible scenarios that
might have attended this child's birth and the nine months preceding it. I wondered if someone held a baby shower for Bill's mistress.
If my husband went to the OB/GYN with her. Got an ultrasound
with her. Found out the gender ahead of time with her. Picked out
nursery room colors with her. The cultural rituals surrounding the
arrival of a baby are so ingrained that maybe they transcended even
the twisted circumstances of this birth. We have a need to celebrate
every milestone.

The old, fat woman stared hard at me in my car and then moved away from the window, into the interior of the house. I am sure she guessed exactly who I was.

It wasn't until two days later that Bill arrived home from Mississippi. We hadn't spoken on the phone since the day of my Finding Out. I had tried to reach him several times, but he would not speak with me. He had relegated that conversation to the homecoming instead. The boys had gone to stay overnight with my sister and their cousins that night. They knew nothing. It was not time to tell them. I had no clue how I would even phrase the news in a way that they could grasp. I needed to see Bill alone first. And then I would have to figure out what to do and he would have to exist in a kind of mannered, patient stasis.

That's not how it happened, however. In retrospect, I would have preferred to have more control. Over myself. Over the situation. Over what was asked and what was answered. But there was no chance of that. I was functioning at half-mast and felt outmaneuvered at every step by a husband who had no intention of explaining himself or sitting with me to talk this over.

Bill came home late at night and stayed no more than ten minutes. I was sitting in a chair in the living room, quietly, with the lights mostly out. I had been sitting there most of the evening, bereft of energy, incapable of focusing on anything but this bizarre reunion. I had no idea what to say. I wanted Bill to speak first. I wanted the luxury of just waiting. I wondered if he would fall on his knees in self-mortification. I wondered if he would ask my forgiveness. I wondered if we would experience some renewed show of devotion. I was so emptied out that I was willing to be filled back up with anything at all.

I saw him walk through the kitchen, look around, scouting for me. I didn't call out. Instead I was aware of a space opening up, much as it had before, between the moment he came into view and the moment he clamped eyes on me. It was a long moment. I looked at him with dispassion. I wanted to see how this level of deception manifested. I wanted to see what it looked like. It looked pale and tired, but simultaneously defiant. And at that time all I could think of was, How the hell did you keep such a thing hidden? There was the smallest trace of awe.

Then Bill saw me and put his coat down. Virtually the first thing he asked was if I had threatened the mistress and the baby. Huh? He claimed she had been getting phone calls. She was nervous, this other woman. Bill didn't want anything like that happening. He said he was concerned about the safety of his child. I thought I was going to be sick. So this is how it would be. His concern shot in that direction first. I should have ended the marriage right there.

Bill went upstairs and packed a bag, although he didn't tell me his plans or where he was going. He just came back through the living room and looked over at me. It was one of the most freighted moments of my life. There was so much to say, and the weight of it stopped all motion. Stopped even time. I didn't know what to ask first, so I asked almost nothing. I had expected that Bill would sit down with me and talk about this. But he didn't. From that point on, he was forever running away. I hated it—not just the deception, but his refusal to confront it with me even when he ought to have felt himself nailed to the spot by the very.

That night, as always, he was impossible to catch hold of. Throughout the ten months to come, we were engaged in this sick game of Marco Polo, an emotional version of the kind we all played in pools as kids. You swim blind and call out, "Marco!" but by the time you have swum over to "Polo!" there is no one there. Bill stroked out from under my questioning at every turn. He was always running, avoiding, arguing his way out of an answer. So the only thing I thought to ask him in that fraught moment was, How did you not know she was pregnant? A stupid, useless question if ever there was one. I have always fumbled the ball on the most important play.

Bill muttered something about kidney stones. She had thought she had kidney stones, and thus the pregnancy went forward unnoticed until it was assured. I think I laughed. Kidney stones. That was her explanation? Honestly, Bill. And that was all it took. I evinced disdain and he bolted into action. He quickly picked up his bag and walked out the door without any indication of where he was going. We did not touch. There were no theatrics. The whole exchange was taut and cold, and then I heard the back door shutting.

I just sat there, more numb than before he had come home. That was it? That was all the explanation I would get? I didn't know what Bill was thinking, but he must have been relieved that the news was finally out and that he hadn't had to tell me. If you remove all the emotion surrounding it, you could see that his was an extravagant deception. It must have been hell to keep it hidden. Some people lie little. Some people lie big.

The birth of his out-of-wedlock child had moved us into a whole new circle of deceit, into that tortured fraternity of women and men, larger than we realize, who are heaved by their loving spouses into the dirtiest of vortices—women who find out their husbands have fathered children elsewhere; men who find out their children are not biologically their own. They go through an exclusive set of agonies for which there is no good news.

In the months after discovering Bill's last affair and baby, I functioned as an animal, barely more sentient than a wolf. Alert to the environment only to the degree that it threatened my children. I wanted to spend most of my time in a closet, rocking. I wanted to lie down and lick the floor like a sick dog. I wanted to bang my head against a wall rhythmically but lightly, for comfort. Strange comfort, yes, but I did not question any device I might use to derail the steady, lurking presence of misery. I was awash in stress.

It blew out my metabolism. I lost nearly fifteen pounds in about two weeks. I didn't eat. I didn't sleep more than an hour or two at a time, and waking would be an instant recognition of exactly where I was. My skin was pale but luminous, as if a soft light had switched on behind it. (Why this was the only time in my adult life that I had perfect skin I will never know, but I consider it highly unfair.) My focus was gone. My mind struggled to get itself around this new reality, and it had me pinging like a small metal ball off all sorts of behaviors in an attempt to minimize my pain. The days kept rolling at me and I just did not feel like doing them. I wanted to be airlifted out of there. I kept hoping a helicopter gunship would appear over the horizon to extract me.

Bill was away more than he was home, and only some of that was work travel. He spent much of his time with Her. There were a lot of American Express bills cropping up later from assorted hotels in our area. A night in Chadds Ford, a night in Princeton. He was always moving. Ducking the tumult. Never spending more than one night in the same place, like Arafat. So that he could not be traced or found. He was impossible to pin to any one spot, or for that matter to any one woman. He had begun months of surreptitiously moving back and forth between me and her, me and her, telling one woman one thing, the other something else. In those early days and weeks, I was too numb to simply call her up and say, What the hell is going on?

Bill never wanted to talk it through. I still find this hard to forgive. I wanted to figure things out and I wanted to do it with him, or at least have an answer about what he wanted to do. He would stay in my company as long as our boys were there because he knew I would not throw a scene in front of them. Neither one of us wanted them to know yet. But once they were in bed, once they were out of the room, once they were at school, Bill would disappear. He would find a way to leave. He was rarely alone with me. And if there was that chance, he simply left the house. He claimed work. Or the need to get gas. Or buy dog food. Or sometimes he just split. In my stupor, I accepted this.

Particularly while he was gone, I tortured myself with details known or imagined. I fitted the pieces of his history together like a wicked puzzle. Everything that had happened over the past few years fell into place, covering up tiny holes I didn't even realize my mind had left open, anticipating the day their questions would be answered.

This led me to recall a night in January 2004 when Bill came home after dinner looking exceptionally pale. He walked into the kitchen and leaned against the doorway, looking at me and the boys in the living room with the most serious expression on his face. I said, "Oh, my God, what's wrong?"

He looked at me for a long time and then shook his head, answering, "Nothing. I don't feel well. I'm sick. I'm going up to bed."

He told me later that this was the night he found out that She was pregnant with a child who would be born that July.

I will say this about humans: We are astonishingly acute in our unconscious perceptions. I remember having as a little girl one of those seminal childhood moments we all have—walking in on my parents in their bedroom while they were fooling around. I was young. I had no clue what fooling around was. But something was so off about their reaction to me, something in their feigned, exaggerated casualness, their sudden shift out of the mood I had seen in their expressions, that I stored it in my head. I didn't know I was storing it. But years later when I was twelve and hearing about sex for the first time in my friend Karin's hallway—in the whispered, grossed-out tones of fascinated young girls hearing an icky new concept—I remembered that moment. I thought, Oh. I see. That's what they were doing.

This is how I remembered Bill's January night. The memory of it came right back. It did a flyby through my consciousness and then dropped right down into that puzzle hole, sealing up the edges between it and the smoother narrative of my life. That odd night in January had been clarified.

I wonder if Bill had planned to tell me then. I wonder if, when he leaned against the doorway, he was thinking: Should I tell my family, should I ease this shocking burden by confessing right now? What a moment this must have been. Compassion rises. The conflict would have been tough to bear. However, Bill chose not to tell me then. I do not know why. Of all the routes he could have taken, that is the one I wish he had not. I wish he had told me of his own accord. I wish I had not found out from friends whom I see every week, people I love and hang out with. The smallest trace of that morning hangs on nearly every get-together.

Part of the reason I had, earlier in our marriage, confessed my affair with Tommy was that I thought it more honorable to come clean, if you could use such a phrase when you are committing adultery. I am not ascribing degrees of badness. But there are routes out of betrayal that attach to more decency.

After sinking so low, coming clean was also a way to recognize myself again, or at least the self I wanted to recognize. The description "adulterer" is not one that most people want to pin to their smocks. Hester Prynne did it and look what happened to her. After that first affair with Tommy, I did not want to have to think about infidelity as my defining characteristic. I wanted to move back in Bill's direction and into my marriage again. Confession was a necessary part of that. I had stormed the sanctuary, and then I wanted to return to it.

But there was also relief in the telling, and that was another motivation. Holding on to and maintaining the DEFCON alert posture that your infidelity keeps you in is debilitating. It's a steady, thrumming chord of agitation that runs through every day and every night. Because you don't want to get caught. Because you don't want to cause pain for your spouse. And, truth be told, because you don't want to be forced into giving up the lover before you're really ready to do that.

When you are newly infatuated with someone, joy and recklessness rule the day. It is not easy to contain such a bizarre fusion, such a hot mix of smashing atoms. They generate an unpredictable plasma. This is crazy enough when you can indulge it out in the open, when every emotion is allowed and you can broadcast your feelings for someone or glow like a samovar. But when you are married and cheating and feeling that emotion for someone else, you don't have this option. You have to keep it hidden. The effort saps

35

most of your vitality, and it saps you. It requires enormous vigilance if you don't want to get caught. And you can tell so few people, maybe none at all, that you feel utterly isolated.

When friends talk to me about infidelity, this is what I say. Finding out about an affair will blow you into a state that is something like post-traumatic stress. Committing one will be a lower frequency of the same, half-deranged state of unease. And that is mitigated only by the few moments of ecstasy you will have in the company of the Other.

One hot summer morning in 1988, I drove to my job at a newspaper in Princeton, New Jersey, with crazy washing through my brain. I had known Tommy for about a month at that point and was with him as often as I could be—after work, before work, on weekday nights when Bill was traveling—but not often enough for me. The affair was in full throttle and I hated having to ease it back and cut short my time with Tommy. My mind was running amok and I gave full rein to the wild notions that arose.

Maybe, I thought, I could just live like this and have them both. Maybe Tommy and I could run off and never be found. Maybe Bill and I could run off and never be found. Maybe Bill will consent to turn a blind eye. Maybe we can all take a house together by the sea. There was nothing rational about the options I pretended were open to me. I was enamored with a man who was not my husband. Rational thought had been jettisoned long ago. In its place rose contemplation of the most idiotic sort.

Desire will do that to you. It takes over your brain. The thrill of newness came flooding back to me from my first experiences of love and sex, and it was as difficult to control then as when I was seventeen. The mere sight of Tommy was enough to send me around the bend. I would see him—hell, I would think about him—and the immediate sensation was of some soft, squirrely creature rolling around in my rib cage, making me feel breathless and boozy and slightly constricted with longing.

It was not just about the sex. It was about the drowning sensations around it—the masculine smell of a new man, the noises he made, the small things he did that made him just him. Bare skin on bare skin. The sight of his bed. The thought of finding him asleep in it. The thought of sleeping in it with him. He had a way of wrapping himself around me so that I was enclosed within the embrace of his arms and long legs, one of them usually thrown over me. I slept that way often, jolting awake a half hour after sex and driving back home stunned with sleep and bummed at having to leave his house.

I drove to work that one summer morning in the crush of obsessive thought. When would I see Tommy again. When would Bill go out of town. When could I find an hour to crawl into bed with my lover and get home in time to wash him off of me. This is not fun. An affair is not fun. It is like a bad habit. It is like addiction. You do it all on the sly, and you steal from your own cupboards to cover the cost. I was crazy with distraction because I knew Bill would be at a client dinner that evening and I had only a small opening in the obligation of marriage. I had to reach Tommy and tell him. But he wasn't answering his phone.

I tried to focus on my deadlines at work, but by midday I was a creature of indeterminate sanity. So I fabricated some excuse to leave. You do this. You act on reckless impulse and hope to unscramble the consequences later on. I left work early and drove an hour to thump on Tommy's apartment door in frustration and in vain. He never showed. I had just so much time that evening to disappear in with

37

my lover and then it would be up. It shrank. Then dwindled. Then blinked out altogether.

I drove home busted and feeling completely trapped by the futility of my behavior. This is one of the places where having an affair is as wretched an experience as having one visited on you. I was thankful that Bill was not there immediately. I had time to regain some sense of my marriage before he arrived home. I accomplished this by doing our laundry, feeding our dog, looking at our photos on the refrigerator, walking through the house itself. The place I lived with my husband. As if I were tossing a grappling hook at some solid structure—the bookshelves, the stair railing—and hauling myself back to my first anchorage. But it was an unhappy evening. There was simply no good end coming, and I knew it. Affairs never end well.

The perception is that committing adultery is at least more pleasurable than having it committed against you. This is only marginally true. One side is not a whole lot better than the other. You should know that going in. The guilt, the divided life, the constant state of cunning, take a toll. It cleaves your world into two parts: half miserable, half bliss. Half pond water, half festival. You cannot share anything between them, and you have to enjoy—or at least refrain from demolishing—the fruits of each in an especially narrow way.

You become very careful about your adulterous pleasures. Good at confining them, tamping them down so they remain in the space you have allotted them—between dinners with your husband or between nights sleeping at home. I rarely allowed myself a long, luxurious swim in the full range of feeling, as the emotions might spill over the levee and swamp the other half. It is the equivalent of clapping your hands over your ears and hearing the whole of your world's sounds through them, as muffled noise. As when I was in Brandywine at that pub, for instance, having drinks with Tommy and playing pool with his friends.

I really did like them. They were fun. They were tough and they were loud. They smoked and drank in equal measure. They ran garages and drove pickup trucks and wore worn flannel shirts with the sleeves cut off. They had mutts for pets. They hadn't gone to college and they didn't care about politics and they didn't care about Dostoyevsky. They didn't know about Dostoyevsky. They knew about trout and lift kits and what kind of beer was on tap. It was a different world from what I was used to. Not better or worse or coarser or more authentic. Just different. Being with them was like visiting another country. I liked it. I found myself laughing a lot. I found myself smoking cigarettes a lot. Someone would yell in my direction that it was my turn at the pool table. My name, Wendy. It floated above the noise and plucked me out.

But in the middle of the small joy of belonging to those loud people, I remember thinking, suddenly, Wait a minute. This is not my life. I don't belong at this bar with Tommy and his friends. This is not my scenario. What am I doing here?

That happened a lot. I would step out of my own reality so completely during an affair that I could forget about it—until something swatted me back. Then I would remember that I had, as part of my legitimate world, a home, a husband, a place with my identity stamped on it. That was my real place, the one known and acknowledged by friends and family and workplace and neighborhood. The one in which I had established my public self. This place at the bar was not mine. The realization ruined the night. It ruined many nights. It proved that living in two parallel worlds made a mess of your mind. I can remember leaving my house for Tommy's apartment on several occasions and feeling nauseated over the deception. Like an amusement park ride with a negative g-force that was roiling my stomach. And yet I always went.

Tommy had a two-room rental above a garage, in the backyard of his grandfather's magnificent Victorian home. That home had been built at the end of the Civil War. It was one of the first in Brandywine to have running water. It had more rooms than a college dorm, some of them small nooks with chairs and lamps crowded into gables and one or two drawing rooms fit for a large company of guests. We spent many nights sneaking through it, trying not to wake Tommy's grandfather, a retired doctor who slept fitfully. I always saw that house in shadows, never with the lights switched on.

But I had to shroud this experience and many others like it. Almost anything I didn't do with Bill had to be quashed during the marital part of my life. You cannot talk about some cool old home you had sex in or what a great afternoon you had when it was spent in bed with someone else. I used to drive by that house all the time with Bill in the car and think, I know the lay of it inside and out. I would gaze longingly, prompting all sorts of pointed questions such as What are you looking at? or Do you know someone who lives there? Questions in the same vein as Where are you going? Who were you out with? Why are you home so late?

In response to these and other threats, I learned to fabricate a credible set of excuses and a credible cast of placeholders. "I think Sarah's grandfather lives there, or someone in her family," I would say breezily. The alibis had to be easy to remember so that I could summon them in a seemingly offhand way the next time the issue arose. This statement will generate no sympathy, but it is difficult as hell to wage an affair. It wears you out mentally. You have to be quick and at ease with your prefab answers when you feel anything but. In spite of that, or because of it, I became a professional liar.

I would be sitting at dinner with Bill or driving to the movies and some image of the day would scroll up through my head unbidden—Tommy pulling off my shirt in his apartment, Tommy smiling at me from across the bar, Tommy handing me the sweater he'd bought me for Christmas. I would forget for a split second that these were not part of my legal activities and move to share them. I would have to snap my own mouth shut just in time. Since almost everything I said could have been a red flag, I had to be careful of everything I said. I filtered each word that left my lips.

While this was difficult enough, the very worst moments were when I was in bed with my husband. Sex with Bill became unwanted by comparison, through no fault of his. It changes utterly from an act of love and passion to an act of crushing obligation. You don't want to be with your spouse. It is not his body that you crave. You cry over his shoulder and he believes it is passion or release that has brought you to that brink. You want to say, No. I am crying because I'm cheating on you and because I want to be having sex with someone else and because there's no good way to fix this. The words hang on your lips. The relief you imagine you will feel in confessing becomes so tempting that you almost blurt it out. You almost betray yourself at the most vulnerable moment because you are desperate not to feel this way one moment more.

Sex fell into two camps: obligatory with Bill, wonderful with Tommy. There was no small gulf between them. The longer I carried this on, the more extreme these camps became. I could not look at either man with a fair, untarnished appraisal. I would have needed to be a different person to accomplish this kindly, to appreciate the beauty of married sex and all its known qualities versus the snapping electrical charge of sleeping with Tommy.

I know that being with one man hours after being with the other was cruel terrain for all of us. I avoided those days of overlap as often as I could without raising suspicion. But there were days when I could not, and the comparison was beyond unjust. Sex during an affair is too good and too heartbreaking. Sex with your spouse is too anguished an opposite. All of it is hung with guilt besides. And don't even bother looking into the mirror after such a day. You hide from the scorch of your own gaze.

Betrayal for me always came down to an unbearable mix of yearning and regret. It was difficult if not impossible to be in any one place with contentment. When I was with Tommy, I was working on my alibi and feeling loathsome. When I was with Bill, I was dying to return to Tommy's apartment and his bed. Everything in my life looked just a little out of register—the furniture, the food in the refrigerator, the dog. I had detached myself from my normal point of reference, and it belonged now to a reality I had abandoned in favor of another man. It's akin to sharks gnawing their own entrails after being gaffed aboard a fishing boat. You gnaw your own entrails. You eviscerate yourself. This is no way for an adult to live.

I began to long for simple, honest comforts that grew out of simple, honest actions—going to the movies without looking over my shoulder, having dessert with my husband, walking the aisles of a supermarket. I wanted the ease of every other couple I saw strolling about in public as if they had nothing to hide. They seemed to fit seamlessly into the groove of their own lives, and they wore it with such calm. I wanted to walk through my own life in that way, unrippled.

To this end, Bill and I had driven to a local supermarket one afternoon. He didn't usually go shopping with me, but this one day, when I asked, he said he would come along. He even pushed the cart, pulling it out of a mash-up of other carts in the parking lot to walk alongside me. It was at precisely this moment that I heard a whooping sound, as of guys hanging out a car window, hollering at passersby. I looked up and there was Tommy in the car just racing past us, smiling at me in a reserved way and not waving. He was with a crowd of his friends.

I'm sure it was an anonymous enough event to Bill—a bunch of noisy assholes screeching around a parking lot, no doubt going to the bar at the far end. To Bill it could have been any crowd of noisy assholes. But to me it was something completely different. Even as the scene was unfolding, I imagined it through Tommy's jaundiced view—the woman he was sleeping with, shopping in the most domestic way with her cuckold of a husband, who at that very moment was walking toward the automatic doors pushing a shopping cart.

I felt terrible for Bill. I felt terrible for the hit I imagined his manhood had taken in Tommy's eyes. I wanted to run after the car, yelling, You are not seeing it right! I don't want you to see him this way! Since I was the biggest emasculator in Bill's world, it may seem hypocritical for me to have cared. But I did. It was an almost unbearably fragile moment, something Tommy got to see through indifferent coincidence. I'm sure that for him it condensed months' worth of impressions into one, hard conclusion. I felt a stab of protectiveness for my husband. The supermarket was an hour of companionship, of domestic necessity, not for Tommy's consumption. And yet I had walked right into the tableau, setting Bill up for a takedown in my lover's flinty eyes.

I endured this kind of rotating emotion—frustration over Bill, concern for Bill, disgust with myself, desire for Tommy—for months on end to accommodate the affair. Until I finally grew sick of the whole thing. It ran through the summer straight up until after Christmas, six months of intermittent and gradually decreasing togetherness with Tommy. It spanned a hot July night of sex in the grass to a few dwindling winter nights at his apartment when it wasn't too cold to go out. That was when I realized it was time to let him go.

After I had confessed the affair to Bill sometime in January, I called Tommy to let him know the jig was up. And over. His response was curt and emotionless and not a little bit self-absorbed. I could hear the very edge of nervousness in his voice, the "Will Bill show up at my doorstep?" question not exactly asked but everywhere implied. It was plain what the affair had been to him—fun, a way to get laid often, and suddenly more complicated than made him comfortable. Hearing about my confession made it a little too real for him. I understood his reaction and felt him a coward both at the same time. I never have one reaction when two or three would serve to ratchet things up even more.

I know the question "Why, then?" arches over everything. It is real stress that burns the hours away. And you are lying. And you give up a lot in return for the pleasure of a few hours together with your lover. So why do it? Because apart from the immorality of it, the question of infidelity teeters on worth. Is it worth it? I did not have a clear answer back then.

It has been many years since I last saw Tommy. If I ask myself this question now—was it worth it?—and I base my response exclusively on the affair with him, my answer is a resounding No.

But Tommy is not the best or the only filter for that question. It was an intense affair, for me, but not overly meaningful. I wanted to be with Tommy, but I wanted to be with him in an abbreviated way. I did not want a life with him. I wanted sex with him. I wanted fun. I wanted him to enjoy my young body and I wanted to enjoy his. There was disequilibrium in my head because of Tommy, but there was not a complete failure of balance. So the larger question of worth outweighed the circumstances.

In the course of time, I would have several more compelling places to look for an answer.

MOST RELEVANT FLAME

T IS A short trip by boat from Bohicket Marina down the creek to the open Atlantic Ocean. We left at dawn, cruising past the docks where the shrimp boats tied up at night, past the muddy creek banks where fiddler crabs waved their single big claws, past the white herons lifting like jump jets out of the marsh grass. At six A.M. Johns Island, South Carolina, was a paint box of colors, a deeply sensual place. This ought to have been my first warning.

Bohicket Marina is a small, insular world of anglers, crabbers, and charter boat captains on a tidal creek twenty-five miles south of Charleston. I began visiting Johns Island and its marina when I was a teenager, the year my parents bought a summer home there. I have experienced every phase of my life through it except early childhood. I was intoxicated with the South. Everything about it was different from my home in Pennsylvania. I was a Yankee there, defined by my Yankeeness. The dock men I knew at Bohicket tolerated but did not necessarily love northerners. I was welcome only because my father was well known at Bohicket and because I love to fish. These excused a host of Yankee sins.

It was early June 1990 and I was on vacation from my job, headed out with a boatload of anglers to the Gulf Stream. The Gulf Stream runs through the Atlantic Ocean off the East Coast, a current cutting a swath of bluer, warmer water from the tip of Florida to the coast of Newfoundland. Because two different temperature zones converge along its edges, it's where the game fish feed. Blue marlin and tuna and mahimahi gobble the rich store of fauna tumbling along its upwellings and its eddies.

Once we arrived at the edge of the stream after a few hours' cruising, we threw in a few lines to see what came up. What came up was an assortment of wahoo, mahi, and, for me, a 120-pound blacktip shark. He hit my line hard and testily, and I sat back in the boat's fighting chair to brace myself and haul him aboard. My upper-body strength has always been dodgy. It felt like dragging an Isuzu truck up out of the depths.

It was this short, nasty contest that presaged the coming of Steven. If I hadn't reeled in that shark, a crowd would not have gathered to see it back at Bohicket Marina. If a crowd hadn't gathered, Steven wouldn't have gotten off his boat to investigate. If he hadn't investigated, I would have gone home without meeting him. And if I had gone home without meeting him, I might have had a different tale to tell.

I always felt that my affairs happened in this slow-motion fashion. Incrementally, inexorably, every step morphing into a whole that drove toward one conclusion. I realized this clearly only after the fact. Looking back, I can see all of the evidence mounting, piling up like a wave, less able to stop, more capable of destruction, sucking up more water as it moves in to shore.

This chapter should come with a caveat. Romanticizing adultery seems an unfair thing to do, but the truth is that it can be transformational on every level. It answers something we crave in our regularly coupled lives and cannot get in the same continuous measure—passion, inspiration, even a ration of joy. At least in the beginning, affairs are like a blast of pure oxygen, so that drawing on the more usual marital cocktail of 78 percent nitrogen and 21 percent oxygen (there are some trace elements) seems a less satisfying draft.

I was twenty-nine when I met Steven. I had been married almost three years and had already run through the affair with Tommy. Although Bill and I had recovered our marriage by simply moving forward after Tommy, there was something of the slippery slope to it. I had already had an affair, so I felt less inclined to stop myself from having another. I thought that this second affair would come to the same sort of end—meaning I would tell Bill about it and then we would just go on as we had before. It was a little like being a teenager again with that dangerous mix of hormone and hubris and thrill of freedom. You never think anything really bad will happen to you.

From the perspective of a whole twelve months, I looked back on Tommy and saw that nothing all that terrible had come of it. Our marriage was intact. Bill seemed to have forgiven me. He would sink into occasional periods of bitter disregard. And of course I knew why. I would respond by sinking into a quieter version of myself, allowing the guilt I felt to acknowledge itself in this way, signaling to Bill that, yes, I am aware of your unhappiness. And I am sorry. And then the mood would change and we'd be right back where we had been. Hanging out. Going to work. Running with our dogs. Inviting friends over for dinner. Making love more or less regularly and occasionally hitting a level of passion and wildness that equaled my need for it.

And so I concluded that nothing all that terrible was going to come of my having another. Even if I behaved like a reckless adolescent. Even if I stayed out all night. Even if I blew that vow out of the water. Even if I did jump off the roof clutching a lighted blowtorch into a pool of knives.

It was a dangerous time in my life, those summers of Tommy and Steven. I had discovered the inconvenience of managing my compulsions. Oscar Wilde tells us that the only way to get rid of temptation is to yield to it. I sailed behind this justification with an arrogance unexplained by any pattern of behavior up to that point. Before I was married, I had been a serial monogamist. I was committed to one man wholeheartedly until suddenly I wasn't. And then I would turn elsewhere for my romantic stoke. But after my marriage, I found my commitment to monogamy ran only about ankle-deep. Sex was part of the allure of affairs, but it was never the whole gig. What I wanted most, what drove me in every affair I had, was the drug and energy of passion, of new intimacy.

I have a few female friends who claim to be able to divorce sex from emotion. They could have one without inviting the other. How they are able to do this is a mystery to me. I have never done it. Maybe it's easier for some people to find a comfortable average between the loose cannon of emotion and the purely physical need for sex. For me there was no dividing them. Sex, love, abandon, passion, all came hand in hand and wild horses couldn't quarter them running in four directions at a gallop.

You cannot in my mind feel only physical attraction for someone who has the power to tempt you out of monogamy. The alchemy of it is too destabilizing to be just about the body. When the attraction arises, it comes from a feeling that this other person is desirable in the most complete way. Not just physically but mind, heart, expression, bearing, voice, right on through to the way they dress, the way they laugh, the way they look at you, and so many other qualities that are not purely physical.

This is why I was so willing to risk things again. From the start, Steven seemed more than just someone pretty to sleep with. I knew there was the possibility that I could be wrong. He could have turned out to be awful. I could have turned out to be awful. But for then, the possibility of new passion was all I could see.

I have tried many times to deconstruct allure. It is the least romantic of tasks, but it is marginally useful, if only to prove a point. When you take attraction apart, when you look back on what developed and how, you find that it is a physical impulse for about eight seconds before it moves on to something bigger. This is why affairs are so crushing for the spouse. Because deep down you know that your husband or wife wanted someone else not necessarily because something is wrong in the marriage, but because someone else was more alluring than you were, than the vows that were taken, than a promise to remain true. Affairs are affairs because of the sex, yes. It would be upsetting but not destructive if your spouse just sat in a café holding hands with someone else. But sex is just the starting point. Sex is what you think you want until you get it, and then you want all the rest.

But for the sake of argument, start with the physical. How Steven looked. He was tan, thirty-five, curly-haired, and sun-streaked, as handsome as a Marlboro Man. His eyes were sharp green, like microdots. There was a sprawl of tiny wrinkles at their corners that suggested a life in the sun and lots of laughter. When he smiled at me, his teeth were as white as Chiclets and his voice all southern honey. His white tank top was off, the top of it tucked into his waistband. It drew my eyes to the flatness of his stomach and the spare line of curly hair starting just below his navel. Oh, I wanted to trace that line.

But I don't know that that would have been enough. The hook was the way he looked at me. His eyes were full of intelligence. A gaze deployed boldly and directly that gave me to know there was a lot behind it. Fun. Good sex. A strong, masculine presence. An equal partner. A full house of confidence. Steven was raised to be that way, and it showed because he was a happy man and because he loved fishing and the confirmation of sharks offshore and the sun out over the dock. And the promise of someone else's young body next to his in bed.

You see? This is what always happens. I start with the physical and I end up somewhere far removed, in the lee of something much less definable. I end up with the mystery of attraction. I start with a shirt tucked into a pair of shorts and end up way past that in territory that determines why we choose this one person and not the other standing nearby. There were good-looking southern men all over that dock. But only one man pulled my focus. This choice is what makes it personal. This is what convinces you to forget that you are married. This is attraction on nitrous. I can deconstruct all I want and I will never tap into the core of it.

When I was standing on the dock, I didn't have this lengthy inner dialogue with myself. My mind had already worked through the calculus moments after seeing Steven for the first time. I didn't ask myself if I hated betraying Bill again. I didn't ask myself if it was love that I wanted or sex. The answer would have been Yes. Yes, I wanted love, or a facsimile of it. Yes, I wanted sex. Yes, this man could deliver. Yes, I wanted to go home with him. Yes, yes, yes.

I swallowed wholeheartedly the drug of attraction. I loved the surge of it moving through me and making every hour leading up to the sex I knew I would have later clear and alive. So that twenty years after that day, I remember the oily smell of that shark on the dock, the thickness of the summer air, the brittle edges of clouds against the blue sky, the sound of pluff mud popping along the riverbanks.

Immediately on standing next to Steven I felt a frisson snapping between us. Some neuron in my brain knocked itself loose and began rapping on my awareness, saying, *Yo, are you still in there? Pay attention. You're doing it again.* I could have hit the kill switch. I didn't. I just ignored it the way I used to ignore my mother calling me in from neighborhood play. Every sense kicked in at full throttle. Sight—gorgeous. Smell—warm cotton. Touch—warm skin. Hearing—deep male voice. Taste—well, salt water and anticipation. It was a very sensual afternoon. I hummed with the energy of it. If you touched my arm, you would have felt the vibration.

From there it was an easy decision to have drinks with Steven at the Privateer Bar nearby. I remember walking there after the shark. I remember rum and lots of it. I remember going back to the boat Steven captained and climbing belowdecks. I remember clothes coming off and the joy of a beautiful, new, well-muscled body and the deep, thrilling awareness of his pleasure. I remember coming awake to music in the boat's stateroom—Robert Cray, of all voices—with Steven asleep beside me. I remember a quickly whispered goodbye and a plan to meet at the dock later the next day. There was no question in my mind that we would both be there.

This new affair cleared the decks for me mentally. I changed all arrangements. I thought only of how to arrange for more time with Steven. Apart from the morality of the whole thing, there were some minor inconveniences to be worked out before another rendezvous.

My mother was vacationing with me down in South Carolina. We had planned to fly home to Pennsylvania on the same flight about a day later. Of course I had already worked out in my mind that that wasn't going to happen. It was just a matter of calculating out to the point of zero how I could stay there without raising any suspicions. I adopted an attitude of insouciant need. I *need* more vacation. I am so stressed at work, I *need* a few more days. I *need* to relax in solitude. I couched my personality in that kind of thinking. And then simply buried the real reason. The appearance conformed to the mind-set all too easily.

The next day, I arrived at Bohicket Marina trying to look casually cool about the fact that many of the people there had seen me leave the bar with Steven the night before. When you are doing something wrong, you are on display. You must send out a signal, some miscreant pheromone. Everyone can sense what is going on. Like I said, it was a small, insular world there at Bohicket. There was always something untoward happening, some unsavory relationship secretly taking shape amid the charter boats and fishing rods and diesel fumes. We just happened to be that week's something. Anglers are no strangers to gossip. I am quite sure my acquaintances at the dock the next morning knew precisely why I was there.

Steven was already walking toward me before I saw him. Smiling. Could not have cared less about the parade of sins we were marching ahead of in broad daylight. The look on his face said, Okay, we're past the need to beat around this bush. How soon can you get away and for how long? His confidence had a riptide effect.

That evening, I had the world's most endless dinner at the marina with my mother and an old friend of hers. I was desperate to get away from them and over to Steven's condo, where we had arranged to meet. Ordering grouper and watching my mother shrug on a sweater in ninety-degree heat was about the last thing I wanted to do. However, dinner gave me the chance to lay out my defection. Knowing full well that my mother wouldn't argue there, I announced rather breezily that I was staying on Johns Island for another few days. That I had called work and gotten an extended reprieve from my boss. That Bill wasn't expecting me home. That I had already arranged another flight. It was all worked out. Would she mind just traveling home alone? I skipped out of dinner a little while later, avoiding her charge of abandonment. I pretended to be invisible in the face of it because that was easier than admitting anything outright.

A line of small, elegant condominiums ran along Bohicket's dock down to the very end, where the tourists and non-islanders somewhat ignominiously kept their boats. I made my way down the boardwalk, savoring those incredible moments before you meet up with a lover who is waiting for you. It was a gorgeous night, the sun just going down over the marsh grass and the river alight with color. I felt completely unfettered. I wasn't. But I felt that way. Behind me, the sounds of the restaurants and the crowds of people grew muffled, heightening my sense of leaving something behind, funneling toward something. Everything on that dock narrowed down to Steven. I found his condo, knocked on the door, and an instant later felt his strong hand on my arm, pulling me inside with a whoosh of excitement.

Later that night, exhausted, I asked him if sex was always an all-night event. Of course, he said. Doesn't everyone have sex this way? I remember cocking my head at him, at this new idea of long sex. Of hours-long sex. Of sex that is exhausting even though you are young and very little exhausts you at that point. I answered him, Ummm, no. Married sex isn't hours-long sex.

This is approximately when Steven had something to say about his own married sex. I can pretend that I hadn't suspected beforehand, but I had. Steven was married. His telling me this in the middle of that night was more confirmation than confession. There had been just enough hint dropped the night before—the use of the pronoun "we," as in "We live in . . . ," or the suggestion that there were children in the picture somewhere. For him. Two daughters. (Mine were still years away.) He hadn't been dishonest with me. He had told me just enough to see if it would dissuade me, and it had not. I didn't react to those hints because I hadn't wanted to. Then, in bed, when they were placed before me incontrovertibly, I had to admit to myself that I knew. I squinted into the dark. And shrugged. It was not so much a shrug of indifference as of, Well, that can't be helped now. There is much more to say about this. I will come back to it. But for that time being, I was unmoved by the declaration of a marriage and children.

I returned to my own house that night and stayed there just long enough to drive my mother to the airport on the other side of Charleston the next morning and put her on a plane. Afterward, from the moment I arrived back on Johns Island, I was alone with Steven. It was, in fact, sublime.

Steven wanted to show me everything that I had never seen from the perspective of a visitor, from the perspective of a Yankee who flew south and drank at the bars in Charleston and hung out on the beach and, apart from fishing trips, never really scratched the surface of that gorgeous world.

We took a boat over to Botany Bay Island just offshore of Johns Island to look for osprey nests. We watched dolphins driving baitfish up the marsh banks. We walked on the beach at night and made love in the sand dunes, although I found that to be a fairly gritty enterprise. We hiked out into a low-country forest, where Steven handed me a pair of sound-amplifying headphones so I could hear the forest in surround sound. The croak of frogs. The snap of branches. The drip of moisture off a tree fifty feet away. We hiked to a hunting shack on the Kiawah River, where a tire swing hung over the banks. I remember Steven dangling from it while I swam nearby. As he gripped the rope, his biceps were wet and brown as chamois against the tannin-stained water. He looked good.

I loved not only the way I felt with Steven, I loved who he was with me, as well. Funny. Smart. Very affectionate, very tactile and not afraid to show it. He was always grabbing me, sweeping me up, touching my back or my hair or my face, reaching for my hand, coming up close to me. There was nothing about him that was aloof or cold. He was a southerner through and through. He told stories of snakes coiled under porch steps and finding World War II mortar shells at Folly Beach and watching hurricanes rake the low country and bird dogs trained up so well that they stayed in the back of a pickup all day without jumping out after squirrels.

He was also deeply considerate with me in a way that Bill had already ceased to be. I remember one evening during that first long weekend when we stopped over at his friend's house to pick up some boat keys. I was hungry when we arrived. Near to faint. Steven's friend sat talking with me while Steven pulled open cabinets and drawers and pantries and handed me without a word and without my asking a bowl, a spoon, milk, cereal. Quisp, I think it was. Because he could see that I was wilting. Just that.

On my last day, we drove down the coast through part of the ACE Basin, a massive wilderness (but with people) of marshes and drowned forests and rivers and hidden plantations. We stopped at the Old Sheldon Church ruins in Yemassee. It was gutted by fire during the Civil War, but its brick pediments were still standing. It was a beautiful but melancholy place, an apt setting for Steven to ask me what I wanted from him going forward. What did I want? My answer was something along the lines of, Whatever you can give me in our constrained circumstances. I remember him drawing me into his arms and kissing me. But reality had been invoked. The whole afternoon from that point had a broody, anxious cast.

The room we slept in that night at our summer home had long before been dubbed the Honeymoon Suite by friends of mine who spent the week after their wedding there. It was a luxury to go into that room with Steven, to shut the door, to know no one would interrupt us. We closed everything else out. The world shrank down to that room and us in it. It is a very odd and wonderful thing to be in a bedroom with a lover you do not know well on the third or fourth night of togetherness. Convention threatens, but in the sweetest way. He has to take off his watch, you have to brush your teeth, he has to close the door, you have to turn out the lights, you both have to take off your clothes, you both have to pull the sheets back. All the things that a real couple might do, only charged with the most rapt attention. You want to watch every second of it. It was precious beyond belief.

I woke up in the middle of the night to the sound of a whip-poor-will bleating in the wet, marshy forest that wrapped our house. Its call was eerie and haunted. I was returning home to Pennsylvania the next day, and I was unhappy, and the whip-poor-will's call drove it all into sharp relief. Steven woke up. He immediately picked up on my mood and without any prompting said, "It's not fair, is it?" wrapping his arms around me. I cried like my heart would crack. Absurd, in retrospect. I had chosen the very man I needed to return home to. But I had chosen this man, too. It did not at the time seem there was a fair choice to be made between them. I stayed awake the rest of that night devouring Steven because I knew that was going to be the last clean access I would have of him.

Where was my husband? you may well wonder. Bill never liked South Carolina. He never liked much that had to do with my family, and in those years we were all about South Carolina. Bill was supposed to have gone with me on vacation but canceled at the last minute and urged me to go south alone. It was the very rope I would use to hang myself.

Bill was in Russia, so the communication between us was limited. He had called a few nights before to tell me about dinner in a massive, empty, red-curtained dining room in Moscow where there were ten work-starved waiters to each diner. Bill was not a dependent soul. He did well on his own. But this image of him sitting alone in that decaying, Soviet-era dining room tore at my pleasure in Steven. It was one of those keening moments when I was aware of how adultery is its own hell. My awareness of Bill, my obligation and my vow to him, was intruding on my extracurricular life. I pushed the image of Bill at his dinner from my mind, actually visualized myself heaving it bodily from my thoughts. This is a requisite of the school of betrayal. You cannot be distracted by the guilt of it or an image of your spouse eating an unsuspecting dinner alone in Russia, or you may well stop.

I think it was this way for Bill, too, many years later. In the winter of 1995—our first son was by then just eight months old—he had all the pieces for betrayal in place. A willingness to commit it. An inability to resist it. A single-focus attraction. The women he thought dangerous were always the same type: the very opposite of me. Pliable, worshipful, quiet.

I have heard brief and scattered reports about how he met the woman who would become his mistress on the train commuting from Brandywine to New York City. From that shard of knowledge—one of the few I have about their early encounters—I can imagine how the whole thing fell out. Oddly, this made it easier to forgive him. I can see his affair unfolding the same way mine did. Starting out with willful oblivion. Ending up in bed.

First, Bill saw someone who was not simply attractive but attractive and unsettling. He forces a meeting with her accidentally on purpose. He offers up his seat. Or asks her the time. Or excuses himself politely as he slides slowly past. He does something, anything, to get into her sight line. Then they talk, and he realizes he's funnier and more charming under her gaze. He likes this. And don't we all.

The next time he's on the train he looks for her. They had both divulged just enough information that each would know where to find the other. A casual mention of commuter times, for example. Something along the lines of, "I like to take the five fifty to Chadds Ford because . . ." Fill in the blank. You can put anything in there. The content matters not one whit. Only the communication of intent.

So then, another day on the same train, there is the self-conscious meeting of eyes, the instant exchange of awareness that he was looking for her and she for him. They sit together then and many times after that. They talk. They laugh. They draw closer. They exchange phone numbers while pretending that this is all very innocent. They haven't done anything yet, but the virus is already mutating at warp speed and they're going to be ill very soon. Eventually they sleep together. And before long they're sick as hell. You see? It's a slurry of moments.

If you want to avoid infidelity, you could do worse than pay attention to your own motivations when you are attracted to someone in your orbit. These moments that persuade you off the path are like a drift of mental snow that gets thicker and thicker until suddenly, right this moment and not before, you realize you are overcome by blizzard.

It happens at work. At the gym. On the train. At the bar. At the other bar. On the dock surrounded by a crowd of people with a dead shark on a hanging scale. There is the first visual of someone, and then there begins a rapid-fire calculation in your brain, the scientific term for which is "thin-slicing," with a nod to Malcolm Gladwell and his 2005 book, *Blink: The Power of Thinking Without Thinking*.

Under the influence of thin-slicing, Gladwell writes, you draw instantaneous conclusions based on any number of cues you are not even conscious of. But some computer in your brain is clacking away. It is actually deciding things for you that will influence your behavior heavily, if not irrevocably. You are not even aware it is happening. Your fingers mentally tap the keyboard as you banter happily, smile, drop just enough evidence to show you're available, lock eyes, touch his elbow, linger when it becomes obvious that the initial encounter is over. That's when you cross the line into a whole new universe. It's no longer so innocent. You know what you're doing now, and you know why you're doing it. You fill out the coordinates. You figure out where to go next. You go there. You wade right the hell in. You enter willful oblivion.

At first this feels like a scramble, but your mind is converting quite elegantly all the data your senses are absorbing. It is telegraphing your interest in a matter of seconds. And it is picking up the return message. The question you have to answer at that moment is, Where will it go from here? If you don't want to get into trouble, you should just walk away. Stride purposefully in the other direction and do not, like Lot's wife, turn around for a look and invite destruction on everyone in your village.

Adultery is a strange world to wade through, a muddled crossing of appetite and impulse. I have tried to figure out the precise moment things would begin to go wrong. I start with one piece of information as a way to crack the code: with, for example, the allure of another man and how it affects me—like a drug. I move on to my relationship with Bill and how by this point it was no longer so engrossing—and how I miss that (we had been married for only a few years but together for about ten). I proceed to sex—staggeringly good during affairs (or why would you bother?). I try to mold some explanation that makes sense. I want to know why I cannot resist.

But every point tackled yields to another question and another. You could chase those until the end of your days, trying to puzzle out the exact moment when you were beyond help. Was it when you met at the restaurant or hotel or dock? Was it when you actually had sex? Was it when you woke up that morning already bored with the drift of the day? You get in a little over your head before you realize it. That is how I have experienced infidelity.

I have watched friends do it as well, blundering along, enjoying the thrill of someone else's attention. Not realizing that they are sinking just a little more into that cushion, into that unkind luxury of desiring someone else and having that person desire you. Those I know who have not had affairs—or who have successfully avoided them—say much has to do with not putting themselves in these situations. This, too, is a mystery to me. I have trouble imagining a scenario in which I wouldn't have been tempted. Not put myself in that situation? Situations were everywhere.

It felt terrible to betray Bill, but adultery also gave me something in return. In the back of my memory, Steven shimmers, evoking a time and a place. The fecund South is the best analogy for all the things I felt when I met him. The pull of the tides, thick southern heat, dolphins breaching, big empty beaches, sea oats and alligators, and the Day-Glo green of marsh grass. It was a massive petri dish where the very cells of adultery multiplied. That is what Johns Island felt like because of Steven. Everything under its influence germinated and grew wild.

I spent one long weekend with him down at my parents' southern home. We were alone there and up to whatever we wanted. The sex was always good, but it was not the only thing I treasured. I also treasured the grit of an unknown person and the cool, blue wash of passion. It occurred to me that I had been in the Honeymoon Suite with more than one man, my husband among them. And the one who made me happiest there was Steven.

Since that first, short week I have been boating many times, once or twice more with him. I had been out on the water before, but not with someone I was newly enthralled with. All the mysteries converged: ocean, wind, depth, steerage. I loved Steven's boat on the water at night, but I also loved the language of it. Shroud and sheet and main. Port and aft and starboard. I learned what it all meant during my adulterous liaison in South Carolina, and I learned it well. I learned it as I've rarely learned anything else. I was at serious attention, deeply mindful, wide awake at every moment. This was time-sensitive material, and I knew it. I would get just so much of Steven and then never any more. Everything was experienced at full tilt.

I'm not saying this to encourage affairs. I'm saying it because it's true. There is your personality, and there is your personality on an affair. I couldn't achieve that level of exuberance without it. During an affair I became infinitely more alive than the domestic self that did the laundry and went to work, even the newspaper work that I loved. If we were all practiced Buddhists and had the concept of mindfulness down even to just an adequate degree—chop wood, carry water—we wouldn't crave all of that extra stoke all the damned time. Every moment would carry its own gravitas.

But we're not. I'm not. I can't raise myself up just on my own motivation. I'm not that high on life that I can manufacture joy out of the quotidian details. Yet when I'm having an affair, I'm on that level all the time. It's an intoxicating place to be.

And it's more than just the discovery of another person. An affair is a revelation of self. Things come to the fore that you had forgotten or that you hadn't declared with any real awareness. As Steven and I got to know each other, I saw the bits and pieces that constitute a personality take shape in me and move beyond the boundaries of sex. I saw a clear image emerge as I introduced myself to this man.

I was someone who loved to read, I told him. Someone who cannot abide a television that is showing baseball. Someone who misses the sound of her grandfather's voice. Who used to love *Ranger Rick* magazine. Who can't hold her liquor. Who doesn't drive all that well but can parallel park like a champ. Who gets violently seasick. Who swoons over Prokofiev's Piano Concerto No. 3. Who loves politics and international newspapers. Who has smashed a couple of friendships along the way. Who loves European cathedrals. Who can't work out the conversion of decimals to percentages. Who doesn't care to.

I also revealed that I was someone who is duplicitous, not entirely trustworthy. Someone who is capable of grand-scale deceit. Someone who cheats. It is a penetrating course on self. Even those qualities that you might not want to know about are in many ways better contemplated under the reflection of adultery. At least in the beginning, the lover provides a tenderer appraisal. It is a more forgiving way to see yourself, that reflection being at least temporarily misted with incomplete knowledge.

Had I taken stock of my infidelity at that early point in my marriage, I would have seen how different those two affairs were. During my first affair, with Tommy, I learned nothing at all resembling wisdom apart from how to drink too much, how to miss work deadlines because of sex, and how to find another woman's hair band in the corner of Tommy's bedroom and pitch a fit over it. I didn't learn any lasting lessons of guilt and wrongdoing. I learned only important steps in infidelity: how to lie casually, how to shower quickly, how to drag friends into the deception. And also how to act as though my other life, my married life, did not exist. But also, and most significant, that a marriage can survive it. The affair with Tommy was emotional because I was high on how I felt when I was with him. I could step outside of my married self and try on another life, one lousy with cigarettes and bars and noise and sex with a man I was not married to. I was a different version of myself, one of all the disparate personalities getting to come forward after hours, way beyond its time.

But Steven was something else altogether. From Steven I learned how much passion you can suck out of a few brief days, and how that can carry your sense of yourself as a more vital human being through the years after. If I needed to remember the romantic woman I had been when I first met Bill and forgotten with him in the intervening years, I could go back to Steven in my mind. I could remember my happiness and try to restart that engine. People talk about this, the rising effect of an affair. Some marriages even improve under its influence, as though the impulse of passion can be transferred. You once again know the answers to questions that might have stalled your union: How do I express myself passionately? How do I close out everything except the person I'm having sex with? How does bed become the whole world to the two of us? These are not specific to affairs. They are like Hemingway's moveable feast. Even for a long-term marriage. Some people say this. I might have said it, too, had things turned out differently.

It was a disjointed affair, though, that I had with Steven. He lived in South Carolina. I lived in Pennsylvania. I had that one long weekend with him in the early summer of 1990, a handful of days in New Jersey when he came up the coast for a visit later that fall, a short vacation even farther south, and another week the following spring when I returned to Johns Island. There were phone calls and letters. But there were no promises of anything more, and there were none sought. Ours was a romance, a fantasy, and it was conducted in a separate realm from the realities of both of our lives.

Eventually, the romance gave way under the weight of trying to conduct it over 740 miles, not ending so much as dissipating. I don't even remember having what you might call a terminating conversation. I missed Steven's love, but I accepted the reality with an almost unprecedented equanimity. We became friends, which had to be enough under the circumstances. All the circumstances—his and mine. And we remained loving friends for years after, although I have not seen Steven or heard from him in more than a decade now.

I remember once hearing a song on Steven's boat that I have not been able to shake. I was standing in the stateroom one morning listening to Robert Cray, whom Steven loved and played constantly when we were on that boat. Cray's song of infidelity, "Right Next Door (Because of Me)," was blaring over the speakers. In it, Cray sings about the mess a woman has made of her marriage by having sex with him. I remember how that song sank through my very pores and how the words were impossible to ignore: "Around midnight I hear him shout, 'Unfaithful woman.'" It was easy even then to cast ahead to the days when that reality could become my own.

I carry these memories heavy inside of me. They are a lasting fever. They make up a part of who I am, how I understand myself. I could not take them back. Had I known everything then that I do now, I might have tried. I might have tried harder to resist what I shouldn't have had. But I don't know where that would have left me, the holes those deleted actions would leave. Nature abhors a vacuum. I worry what I would have used as fill.

It is easy to persuade myself all these years later that I was in love with Tommy and with Steven and that is why I did what I did.

But it is just as easy to persuade myself that I was not. I see it as a pointless distinction. When I look back, these affairs seem now to be all sorts of things they were not at the time. Now I see them as reckless and dangerous, however much they moved me. Then I experienced them as irresistible, dramatic, and passionate. I did not want to give up any of them, or my husband, either. I simply wanted what I wanted. I didn't wonder if I was in love. I didn't waste any time at all on classifications. I was engrossed in the affairs, each one of them, because of their power, not because I intended some long-term relationship. So I didn't have to bring traditional definitions into the equation.

But I went with Tommy and I went with Steven as if I were in love. Meaning, wholly. Body, mind, heart. I must have been a veritable storm of a woman—everything up front and then sooner or later I would blow over. And turn my attention back to my marriage.

If I push aside all that is dishonest in what I have done—just for a moment, just to capture all parts of that territory—I can take a romantic view of affairs. I do see them romantically. They were a long time ago for me. I see them as exotica. Ireland has its fairies and elves to give it reprieve from a too-careful reality. Scotland has its lochs full of monsters. Japan has its *yokai*. Chile has its Recta Provincia, a government of warlocks who convene in caves. In the absence of a healthy mythology of dwarves and witches to keep my imagination cracking, I threw my weight behind the mystery of attraction. Unless you want to count the great fables of organized religion, there are only the mysteries of Santa Claus, love, and death to catch us unaware.

Affairs are like a seventh day. They are a break from all duties and obligations and responsibilities. I'm not saying this is right and

I'm not saying it lightly. This is just how they are. You can't be responsible when you're with your lover. That would be responsibility's polar opposite. And since you already know you're way out of line, you go the extra distance. You throw yourself in headfirst. You become the very personification of irresponsible. You are way alive, however. Every detail sings. It would be a great way to live if it weren't so ruinous.

HOUSE OF MIRTH

WHAT DOES A couple with such an enormous smash showing on the horizon look like in the beginning? Indistinguishable, of course, from all the other young couples who emerged from college hand in hand. Your neighbor's kids. The young suits on the elevator. The man and woman walking a puppy. Your gay cousin who just moved to Brooklyn with his lover. The liberals. The conservatives. The guys who drink whatever's on tap. The couple who write their own vows. The couple who reject a large wedding and get married instead in Hawaii at the foot of a volcano's shaggy green flanks. We all look kind of similar in the aggregate.

There are no telltale augurs of infidelity or, for that matter, any of the other phenomena that will tank your union, at least none that a twenty-one-year-old would give any credence. It is not so obvious as a facial deformity or a scarlet birthmark or the number of the beast tattooed on your scalp. There are no politics to infidelity. It's not genetic. It's not gender-specific. It's not even predictable. So what did Bill and I look like? Every other Tom, Dick, and Jane.

In the fall of 1980 when I was a sophomore at a university in Pennsylvania, my roommate and I lived in a coed dormitory. The people who ended up on our hallway struck me mostly as not having a whole lot in common with one another. There were a few smart misfits who hadn't found another dorm to live in. There were refugees from fraternity housing. There were my roommate and me, who had picked the dorm because it had the best access to the rest of campus. And there were Bill and his friends, including J. D., a bold and charming Texan who became my friend as well.

All of us moved onto that hallway, scanning the ranks for possible hotness among those who'd be living in convenient proximity. Right away I noticed Bill with his tanned, manly legs and his cutoff sweatpants. I felt something sexual stir at the sight of him then. I don't know exactly why. He looked kind of tough, rumpled, different from the luxuriant crop of preppies who filled out the rest of the university's ranks. Edgier, more street-oriented. Like someone on a Bruce Springsteen album cover. I didn't rush in. We would be living about five feet from each other. The situation needed a light touch. But there was something of a tidal pull to Bill right from the start.

A few months later during Parents Weekend, I saw Bill's mother standing with him in the courtyard beneath our dorm rooms. They were unloading some furniture for his room and she was behind him, talking. She casually put her hand on his shoulder and he reached up and touched it, just for a moment. It was the simplest movement, small and economical. But it spoke volumes to me then. It was as if I could see in that tiny gesture what it was that Bill valued—warmth, human contact, a respectful and loving relationship with the formative woman of his life. Perhaps I read too much into it, but that is what you do when you're falling in love.

By early spring we had had a few dates—movies on campus, late night snacks in the student center, a party at a local bar where we kissed for the first time. We were moving in what seemed to me to be a Direction. I made sure Bill got invitations to parties my sorority threw. I sent him anonymous misshapen romantic cookies of the kind our dorm was always churning out for fund-raising. I declined invitations to go out with other men. I tried hard to seem casual and breezy on the hallway, although I was increasingly nervous around Bill because I liked him. I just didn't know how much until the April afternoon I saw him running up the steps into our dorm.

I spotted him out of my window when he abruptly lost his balance, tripped up the last three steps, and fell against the door. I gasped. I mean, literal gasping. I remember the sound I made. Like in the movies. Like Dorothy when the house sets down with a bump in Oz. "Oohh!" That is how I knew. That sudden flight of concern was so unmistakable that thirty years later I can remember it with perfect clarity and trace an awareness of my love for him to that moment. So, simultaneous with Prince Charles courting Lady Diana Spencer, but with less pomp, I courted Bill.

I hung out at his fraternity when he was there. I spent a lot of time talking with his roommate and with him in their shadowy room with the really bad decor. I made a point of being on the hall when he was on the hall. I consulted J. D. in hushed tones so frequently that Bill asked him one day, "What, are you going to marry that girl?" To which J. D. replied, "BillyBoy, you're gonna eat those words."

What exhilarated me most about romance at college was the license of it. There were no parents around to wreck our amour and to prevent us from sleeping together. This was astonishing freedom. My parents hadn't been draconian, but they had been watchful and mildly disapproving of past boyfriends. They got in my way, as parents will do. At school there were no barriers apart from the ones laid down by roommates. And those were easy enough to circumvent.

That spring, Bill crept into my room most mornings after my roommate had left for class and I was still sleeping, blowing off yet another early English tutorial. I would hear the movements of him—the door opening, the shucking of clothes, the sound of my wooden loft bed receiving his weight as he climbed up to me. It was all delicious anticipation. I remember him once climbing into bed and holding the covers up, as if he were looking at a fully naked woman for the first time and for as long as he wanted.

Apart from Professor Fell's philosophy courses, gravity was difficult to come by on that university campus. Particularly with Bill. He was casual, laid-back, an even flame to my reckless burn. He was not affectionate and he was not demonstrative. I am both, in spades. I suppose his aloofness appealed because it was the opposite of my approach. Anyway, I was only too happy to fill in the blanks for what wasn't apparent in Bill's behavior toward me. One night Bill took a shortcut to my apartment across campus through the local graveyard. He saw there an old woman, bent over one of the tombstones, who did not look up at him. When he arrived at my room, he was disturbed by the encounter—not with fear but with wonderment, almost awe. Whether she had been real or not. What she was doing there so late at night. Why she had seemed so insubstantial. It brought another dimension into our cloistered world of beer and term papers and sex. The weight of his response was intriguing to me. It was that whole "still water runs deep" thing, which, looking back, I can see that I invested way too much faith in. I remember making love to him that night as though we were out of all time.

After our graduation ceremony in the spring of 1983, I stood next to Bill holding my mortarboard and crying hard into his shoulder while my parents looked on in annoyance. They hadn't considered how serious this was. They had met Bill several times but had by their indifferent postures hoped to shush him away. They were WASP-crusty, just a little bit snobby. Bill was poor. Unpolished. I could see from their failure to take to him that their feelings ran to No.

As for me, I was sure the end of my world was coming. Bill would be going back to his parents' house in White Plains, New York, for his first job at a carpenters pension fund outside Manhattan. I would be moving to Boston for my own first job at an advertising agency on Boylston Street. I did not yet realize how easily you could crush distance with cars and trains and phone calls, or the lengths we would go to in order to be together. I simply did not want to be separated from him for any period at all.

In the fall of 1983, I moved up to Boston to live with a girlfriend in a hovel hard by Mass General Hospital's parking garage. It had two rooms and a scary, soiled-T-shirt-wearing landlord. That place was as ugly as they come but it was cheap. Bill and I saw each other only about once a month, not nearly enough for young people in love. But oh, those weekends. We would spend hours and hours in bed and then hours wandering around Boston—Bill most decidedly not holding hands—and then hours more in bed. Sex with Bill in those early years was always good. It was a whole world for us, our reconnection, our confirmation. It was great not because either of us was a maestro in bed, but because we were happy in our choice. When Bill left Boston on Sunday evenings, I felt bereft. Our apartment became disanimated, museum-like in its unnatural stillness. The way a house feels when the electricity has gone out.

After just one year in Boston, I moved back to my home in Pennsylvania. It was a return migration, a Bill-ward route. I wanted to anchor myself nearer him so I could go up to his home in New York as often as possible. I got an apartment with another friend, a job with a weekly newspaper, and a comfortable new rent. During my first week at that job, I drew responsibility for seven stories and was faced with writing them all on deadline. I was mayhem itself. I had no idea what I was doing. Bill drove down from White Plains to sleep next to me and my typewriter while I worked through the night, sweating each story but comforted by his closeness.

Bill proposed in December 1986. We were both twenty-six years old. He pulled the ring from his pocket in my attic bedroom and rushed through the words as if he were learning a new language and was worried about pronunciation. I remember that his voice was shaking. I always wished I had had access to his interior monologue prior to his proposal: why he wanted to marry, what led to his decision, when he bought the ring, why he was so nervous when he knew I loved him. Right back to the beginning, there was never enough revelation in our relationship, never enough said. But then, it didn't yet matter. I answered Yes, with tears. We drove like mad over to my parents' home afterward to tell them the news. They sweetly and somewhat resignedly served us champagne and toasted our future.

If you ran a sword through our marriage on most occasions it would have come out clean. While this might defy belief, to me it seemed a good union in some if not many ways. Our honeymoon still comes back to me as a week of infinite possibility. We had our heads in the wind, no parents or college or schooling or trappings of youth to confine our lives. It was all up to us now, and that was a great freedom. We were free to be adults. We ended up lasting for twenty-six years altogether—eight of them as young lovers, eighteen of them as husband and wife.

Bill was not much of a romantic; he was just enough of one to keep it occasionally interesting. A utilitarian romantic, and so that worked, for a while. He did birthdays and anniversaries and holidays well. What I got from him was always a thoroughly considered present: a birthday cake with Toblerone chocolate bars bricked over the top; a telescope for the backyard because I loved looking at the stars; a vase full of sunflowers to recall our trip to Italy. It served as a reminder of how well he knew me, and I found in that a measure of reassurance.

But as the years went by, I came to understand the real reason I loved Valentine's Day and birthdays and Christmases. Not because of the celebrations themselves but because they were occasions when Bill was almost culturally required to express his feelings for me. The occasions I could count on hearing something loving. He was not affectionate and he was not expressive. "I love you" did not come easily to his lips. He was not warm. Over our years together, this began to tell. We were once walking down a street in town at night in the middle of winter. I said, "I'm freezing." He said, "Walk faster." I thought it was a clever remark then. Now, I see it as incipient scorn.

We lived first in an apartment in New Jersey and then bought a home in the Brandywine area of Pennsylvania. There we became a very social couple. We had friends over a lot. We traveled a lot. We had dogs, we had a lot of stray people crashing over, we argued politics, we had a lot of energy. Our early photographs show us always doing something—camping, skiing, rafting, traveling. We went to

Austria, to the Caribbean, to Alaska, to Italy. It was a breathless early marriage, full of life, seven years of it before our first child was born.

In early 1993 we spent a Christmas holiday in Austria, with New Year's Eve in Vienna. The city that night was crazy with young people. Crammed into a bar there, we met an Austrian couple— married for a few years, childless so far like us, apparently teetering on the edge of the faintest boredom with each other. We hung out with them for hours until Bill pulled me away suddenly. They were looking to swap out for the night, Bill told me as I gaped obliviously. The husband had whispered an offer to Bill over spiked wine, and Bill was furious. So we took off, disappearing into the crowd on the Stephansplatz, with me swooning under the pulse of Bill's territorial response. It meant I was his, he was mine. A fact that we did not often assert but that I found thrilling when we did.

I can still feel moved by this twenty years later. Divorced couples try to maintain at least a shred of respect for their former spouses. They say, He or she is the parent of my children and I will do it for that reason. This statement brings me down. I always feel defeated after hearing it. As if that's the only reason there is to err on the side of slack toward this person you once loved, slept next to, cried over, made love to, bought presents for, married. I also think it's a lot of heavy webbing to drape over the kids, as if you're offering your tolerance as some hard-earned prize: See how I sacrifice for my children by continuing to endure that freak show that is the other parent?

I always hope there is more to it. This is a person, after all, whom we pluck out of a crowd of possibilities. Magic attends that choice. Or if that word belongs too irrevocably to the World of Disney, then use the word *mystery*. At any rate, it's a remarkable kind of calculus that makes you look at a field of men or women and quickly zero in on the one person who turns you on most. He could be standing next to someone better looking, smarter, more athletic, richer, in possession of a more interesting physiognomy or at least better hair. And yet it's a rare day that you spend much time on the question "Which one?"

You have already decided. Through some mysterious alchemy, you want this one and not another. Why? I think a definitive answer would ruin it. There is no reason all our rules of attraction have to be reduced to dopamine surges or serotonin receptors or reproductive necessity. I'm not saying these are not legitimate or even occasionally fascinating. But biological imperatives can foul the mystery in which there is solace and even beauty. Something—something not me—is orchestrating this attraction at least part of the time. And that is a strangely reassuring thought.

The early years of our marriage were filled with making a home and with burgeoning careers. I wrote for Princeton-area newspapers. I was content with covering political tempests and school board scuffles. As long as there was yelling involved. I loved interviewing. I loved entering into other people's lives. The mayor of Princeton at the time, Barbara Boggs Sigmund, was the daughter of two U.S. senators. She was colorful enough to fire up a whole town, so perhaps that's the reason. And there were glittering university luminaries to be profiled at every turn. Joyce Carol Oates. Cornel West. Robert Fagles. Toni Morrison. George Kennan. There were also traces of Albert Einstein's residency, and J. Robert Oppenheimer's, and Richard Feynman's. It was enough.

Bill, on the other hand, was ambitious. He started out on Wall Street and rose amid the ranks of ego and self-aggrandizement, displaying, quite frankly, none of this. Which was part of his success. All those bankers and CEOs and company heads met him and thought, At last. Someone to trust on Wall Street. Ironic it may be, but I don't deny it. Where business was concerned, they could not have placed their trust more solidly. Bill struck me then as almost noble in the way he conducted himself on Wall Street. He progressed from pension fund management to mergers and acquisitions at a storied Wall Street bank. He did very well there. In turn, that bank acknowledged this by sending him all over the world, a career path that had a hand in all this.

What the pretense of on-the-job travel did was obvious. It gave Bill a place to hide and a context to hide in. That context was, I cannot be questioned if I am out contributing to the household both of us are living in; I am away, working hard. So you are not allowed to bother me with suspicion. How well it succeeded. Until suddenly it didn't. And I found out in the spring of 1994 about what I assume was Bill's very first affair. The one long before the one that brought us down. The one with an actual stripper whose club name was Mercedes or Mercator or Chastity Belt or something along those lines.

I was in the kitchen that night making dinner for us when I heard Bill coming up our basement steps. I reached around the refrigerator—it was a very small kitchen—and pulled open the door for him at the top of the stairs. I think it surprised him, the sudden sweep of the door opening. He looked surprised, anyway. And he smelled oddly. He smelled of cigarettes. He didn't smoke. I didn't smoke. It is a scent that cannot be mistaken. When he walked into the kitchen redolent of Lucky Strikes I stopped him and asked, Why do you smell like cigarettes? He looked at me sheepishly and said he had been out to dinner with a woman.

Meeting my incredulous stare, he explained in a rush of innocent-seeming words that he had made a new friend. They had met on the commuter train. He enjoyed her company but nothing romantic had happened. They had just gone out to dinner once. That's where he had been. I didn't need to worry, he said. But he looked sort of twitchy. Guilty. Of something. My brain rapidly began its parsing of data, thin-slicing madly. By this point, I had been an adulterer three times. I knew how one acts, and it looked exactly like this. There wasn't much I could say that would cover both my shock at the likelihood and the accusation of hypocrisy that he would almost certainly level at me.

I can remember deciding almost instantly to take as neutral a stance as I could in the way that people are advised to act calmly in the face of a charging bear. Probably I just didn't want to know. I thought if I ignored it, the reality simply wouldn't take shape in my mind. I did tell Bill that this wasn't cool, that I knew better than anyone how easily things can get out of control. And that I would really prefer that he not go out to dinner with this woman again. I wanted to be calm. I wanted not to make a big deal out of this so that we could go right back to being us. But I said it with enough edge to indicate something else: *Don't* go out to dinner with this woman again. Bill tried to pull off a casual jocularity that did not sit well. It seemed forced and anxious. He assured me there was nothing going on. I did not believe a word he said. We went to bed early that night and fell asleep after a tense détente.

Our relationship hung in that mode for a few days. Bill's efforts to appear nonchalant were increasingly pinched. The more I looked at him, the more I considered the way he moved or talked or looked away from me, the more I suspected him. When he left for an out-of-town business meeting the following week, I was all over it. I began rummaging through the house. I didn't know what I was looking for. Solace, I suppose. Proof that there was nothing there. Proof that their dinner had just been some stupid reflex of temptation rather than a fulfillment of it. That is what I had hoped to find, in whatever form it existed.

It was not what I found. What I found instead was a leather-bound journal in Bill's closet, tucked in under his shirts. The fact of its existence was unusual enough in itself. Bill had never been given to reflection, much less to keeping a diary. But infidelity always needs a confessional. That journal, apparently, was his. I opened it. I ought not to have, but I did. Because I knew it would answer my suspicions. I read only a few entries on the first page. They were short. And dated. The one cauterized in my memory said, "Met a girl. Named Anne," and was dated in August. I was reading the journal in April.

Two days after finding this out—after calling Bill on the phone at work, after having their affair confirmed, after telling him to come home from his business trip and deal with this in person—the phone rang in my kitchen. When I picked it up, there was a pause on the other end of the line. I said, "Is this you?" What I meant was, Is this you, Anne? Because I knew it was Anne. It just seemed like the kind of thing the Other Woman would do—call her lover's home to talk with the wife. It was simply too coincidental to suddenly receive a crank phone call. The person on the other end hung up. And then abruptly called back two minutes later, saying, "Yes, it's me. It's Anne."

During that phone call, she confided that she was crazy about Bill. That they had been together for some months. That she was married and had two daughters. That she was an exotic dancer. A stripper. Whom Bill had met down in Philadelphia the year before when I was away for my little sister's bridal shower. That he had frequently spent time with her that I thought had been spent at the office—weekends, evenings, afternoons. She told me what a gentleman he was. I begged to differ. Strippers. Cheating. Lying. Doesn't sound like the makings of a gentleman to me. Then I asked her to leave us alone. For good.

I can't help but admit that I was shattered. Even though I had had my own affairs. Even though I had done this already. My husband had lusted after someone else. In those interstices between work and home and weekend chores and business trips. Whenever a liaison could be crammed in. While I was home and unsuspecting. The full irony of it was not lost on me. It just came at me with double force, because I had done all that myself, and I knew what was involved. How much was involved. And now Bill had done it back. What a pair we were.

We recovered. There were a few months of feeling like hell. The marriage was for a while thin and insubstantial, as though it could hardly support its own weight. I cried a lot. But I also tried very hard. For me, recovery was not about forgiving Bill. I always forgave Bill. I had had affairs, too—forgiveness was an instant reflex. Perhaps this is why he thought the affairs could continue. Perhaps that is true for both of us. I did not want the marriage to end. So recovery was about feeling shitty and learning to live with it until, over time, it dissipated. But again, there was no reflex on my part to end the marriage. I simply did not want to. We were husband and wife, and this was one of those bad times I had vowed to marshal through.

But once our first son arrived about a year later, things between us began to divide irrevocably, like landmasses pulling apart and sending out all manner of seismic adjustments that would later result in a tsunami. Without realizing it we took our inspiration as parents from the concept of tag teams. This only increased when we had our second son. I did my thing with the boys until Bill came home and then he took over and then I did my thing elsewhere and then when I came home he split and did his thing and occasionally we would meet in the middle before heading out in separate directions all over again.

We were a family on the weekends. But never, as I think back, never for huge stretches of time. Bill was away a lot. And as I would find out in the future, it was not always for work. Frequently it was to be with someone else. He would offer to run errands and be gone sometimes for hours. I could see him getting antsy sitting around the house. Like a shark, he had to be always moving or the gills would stop working and he'd die for lack of oxygen. He was not the sort of father to play with his sons. Did not coach sports or toss a football or run sprints with them in the backyard. When home he mostly stared at his computer, which even the boys came to hate as a false barrier between him and them.

Still, I was not an unhappy wife and mother. And while I don't know what Bill would say now, ours seemed to be a happy house. A good house. A house that did what it was supposed to do. A house for boys. Which I realize confounds explanation in the face of all that adultery. It was life as it happened, not as it was planned. As far as I can tell in looking back, there was no plan. I do remember at about this time getting a solid piece of advice from my sister-in-law. We were in Providence, Rhode Island, with Bill's family. She and I were sitting on the beach while our babies played nearby. Coping with some strains in her own marriage, she told me that she had a simple way of getting around the tension with her husband: that you should always be polite with each other and that you should always have sex when the other wants it. Because sometimes manners and sex are all you will have. And that, she said, is enough to get you through the worst of it. I liked that advice. I do still. I am a great vacuumer up of advice, sucking all of it in and ejecting what makes no sense or what doesn't fit into my life. This fit. I practiced it for years.

The roommate existence went on. Because the gap was easing apart only incrementally, it was not apparent that it would set up to be a problem. I liked it. Obviously so did Bill. But I see now that it was the very pattern that allowed betrayal to go unnoticed for so long. I had close friends who barely knew Bill. He was often identified around our neighborhood as "Wendy's husband." The boys and I traveled on our own frequently, usually down to South Carolina. It did not occur to me to observe a more traditional family dynamic in which you more or less assume togetherness.

Of all those I know well enough to draw conclusions, I can describe six friends as really great parents, all of them from my neighborhood and local elementary school. I realized when I was tallying impressions in my head that these people scrolled up as coupled entities. And I do not mean simply married. Most couples operate along the divide-and-conquer matrix, with the wife doing this part of the work and the husband doing that part and resentments over the imbalance accruing over the years like estuarine sediment. I love the way these six people think, act, work as a family. As one solid unit. It works. But it was completely alien to our own arrangement.

When I was in sixth grade, a boy in my class walked up to me on the playground and handed me a Snoopy Valentine's Day card. In it he wrote, "I love you." I was instantly smitten. Smitten with him because he was smitten with me. It really was that simple and arbitrary back then. We started "going out," and that was our tag on the playground. It was a new status for me. I loved it and reveled in the sense of couplehood, even then. Until I saw this boy try to catch a baseball one afternoon and slam clumsily and with bloody, stentorian consequence—"I need a tissue!"—into another boy. It was suddenly over. I realized what it is like to feel a creeping repulsion for someone you once adored, even if it began only five minutes ago, even if you are only twelve. I was in relationship training from that point on, astonished already at how fickle attraction could be.

I had a rubric for relationships. For what they should do (send me to the moon and beyond), how they should make me feel (ecstatic at all times), what I was prepared to put in (what wasn't I prepared to put in?). But I did not conceptualize marriage. It needed its own rubric because it was a long-haul deal and because passion breaks down over the years, whereas it rarely gets to that point in earlier relationships. When those failed to inspire, you just moved on. Not so with marriage. I had never wondered what it would feel like over many years or what would be ideal. I assumed marriage would unfold for me in much the way it had for my parents. Meaning—well, luckily, happily. We were married. I didn't think about it much beyond that point.

But married love for the two of us followed the same somewhat dispiriting trajectory many marriages follow. There was a storm of attraction, passion, and love followed by calm, followed by too calm, followed by Hey, can we get some passion around here? Spread over many years, that lessening of intimacy became tolerable because life was naturally being built around other foci. Children. Home. Work. How did I characterize the view then? Boring. Satisfying but boring. I didn't imagine that was unusual. An exciting marriage was not a priority. The boys were. One night in the fall of 2000, the three of us were downstairs ready for bed, all in pajamas, when the dogs started leaping around, signaling Bill's arrival home. The boys and I threw ourselves under a huge blanket and lay on the couch, giggling, waiting for him to walk in the door and discover that odd lumpen object. The boys were ecstatic as Bill wandered around the house, calling out for them in seeming perplexity. I could hear in his voice that he was laughing.

It is important to point this out. Because apart from the infidelity the marriage wasn't terrible for me. I cannot answer for Bill here, but I did not run to another set of arms because I was beaten or bereft or even plain old unhappy. None of this was comprehensively so. In pieces, yes. There were many disappointments, and there was neglect. But overall. No. I deprive us both of those singular justifications for good reason, because I do not want to cloud the picture with faulty rationalization.

Quite apart from that, I don't want to annihilate my past with Bill. The four of us—Bill, me, our sons—are more than just the patterns through which the marriage ended. That is just a part of the story. Like everyone else, we as a family present more along the lines of what author John Fowles once described as "the sum of all its phenomena." Not just the mess of conclusion, but the pleasures of daily life before it, too. I am grateful above all for our sweet sons. I am grateful for Bill's early love. For our honeymoon. For his partnership in the beginning, daunting phase of adulthood. For his intelligence, because he was wicked smart. For his sarcastic humor. For the way he used to look at me. I am grateful for Montana, for Providenciales, for Alaska—all memorable trips that we took after my affairs and before our children that come back to me as perfect moments in the life of our marriage.

In Montana, I drove my snowmobile off a thirty-foot cliff in Yellowstone Park and was lost in the snow for a good twenty minutes. I could hear Bill's snowmobile ripping back and forth on the cliff above as he yelled for me. When he found me—I was fine, although my snowmobile was mortally wounded—his face was pale with worry. That night driving back to our hotel, he pulled me close and drove with his arm around me. Like all those high school lovers you see driving around locked against each other despite the obstacle of seat belt and steering wheel.

Years later in the waters off Providenciales, a friend yelled that he'd seen a shark circling beneath us as we were snorkeling. The friend swam toward the boat, leaving me sputtering and panicky, alone in the water. As I tried to get myself together, I dropped my face mask. I dropped my snorkel. One fin came off. I think I wet myself. I couldn't get any closer to that boat. Bill, who was closer, swam away from it to me. He could see that I was in a panic. Until I saw him coming. There was sublime honor in that rescue.

And Alaska? Oh, Alaska. We went there with a couple of college friends some months after I had confessed to having an affair. After a long trip of wet sleeping bags and blackfly molestation and sea-kayak nausea (it was perfect), we ended up the last night at a ramshackle hotel in Cordova. There, able to make love for the first time in a week, Bill and I reunited in the best of ways. I remember that when he turned toward me in bed, I asked him, "Am I still your wife?" And his reply: "Always."

It's easier to sift through all the years of travel to locate moments of real joy among them. Context is mnemonic. The domestic life is overwhelmed by so many details that much of its beauty gets obscured. Like the layers of sea ice scientists take core samples from, drilling down thousands of feet into the frozen plates around Antarctica in search of evocative debris. After many years of marriage you take stock in just this way, drilling a deep vertical hole. All those meters of bland, white ice are striated with sweet detail, and these come forward, glittering like mica.

I'm just not any good at remembering them on my own unless persuaded by loss or contextual memory. What is immediate and accessible at all times is the frustration. And the mind—so discursive, so noisy, so obnoxiously nattering on about how inadequate your spouse is—feeds right into it. It barks and barks of injustices being committed right here, right in this house, right before your eyes. What boggles me now is how the domestic gets lost in its own definition. It becomes, like the idea of a safe marriage, a bore. A sign that something is wrong.

I don't know how much of Bill's adulterous behavior was tripped by my own. I assume I started it, although I will never know for sure. If it was comeuppance I deserved for that, it was comeuppance I would get in spades. I wonder if I deserved, though, this level of betrayal. It is a fair question, one of many I could ask about our marriage going back and back through the years as I trace the source of our dissolution.

I once asked Bill if he thought my infidelity had made a difference to his own. If it was the initial shot fired that put him on his own path of betrayal. I remember him pausing to think this over. And then he said, with a sad smile, No. This was a great kindness. Permission to *not* shoulder all the blame. It is one of the things that allows me to look back with poignancy at the flawed individuals we were. These are all part of the complexity infidelity coils around you. If you can understand it, you can forgive it. But it's really simpler than that. If you can understand, you can understand. I can see how it all fell out for Bill because I know how it all fell out for me. There is nothing like an unobstructed view. My own earlier practice of adultery gave me this view. I do not think it would come as easily to someone who has simply been a victim of a spouse's betrayal. The compassion you feel toward your own motivations for betrayal can be extended to someone else. And should be.

How would I characterize the view now? Safe. Married love of the best kind is safe love. This is not revelatory. But each new couple comes bang up against this quiet street without really expecting to, and the shock of recognition—have we really arrived *here?* just like everyone else? where did all that passion go?—is in many ways fatal to the relationship. I did not know how to live with the idea of safe as opposed to dramatic, because I looked at safe as boring. As in failure. As in dead.

Maybe what I needed was a new way to think of the drama made manifest in safety. I would get that in spades, too.

During the month after Bill moved out, I woke up often in the middle of the night. The fact that I was there alone and unused to it was unusually scary. I was always a chicken in the dark. I think I saw *The Exorcist* at too young an age. (Or really at any age.) What I wanted was someone warm and loving breathing next to me at night. It took a long time to get used to this loss. To the knowledge that the house held one adult instead of two.

At those times safe didn't feel boring. Safe felt like a rescue. Safe felt like the most romantic, knight-on-a-horse, warrior-brandishing-a-sword existence possible. Not because I was insulated from trouble when in a couple, but because I was facing it with someone. The way big, friendly dogs back their tail end up to you and then *lean*. That's an instinctive gesture of fraternity. It says, You have my back while I scan the horizon for dragons. As competent as I feel as a woman and as modern a definition as I apply to myself, feeling safe is one of the gifts of being a social animal. Safety in groups, in numbers, in a couple. Safety of the primal sort. Of someone having your back.

This is not hindsight. It's serious, keening, howl-at-the-moon regret over not recognizing the luck that surrounded both Bill and me. The sound of my husband sleeping. The cut and cottony smell of his T-shirts in the laundry. The daily, reassuringly impartial inquiries of people in my hometown: How is Bill? How are the kids? How are you? The sound of his car door slamming shut when he got home from work. His innate wisdom operating on life's perplexities. The sight of him swimming toward me in shark-infested water. These are the details of married life. You could slay a dragon with them. What a pity that we missed the most salient point of union, that we fell prey to the most obvious stupidity—not knowing how good it all was.

My husband is a mystery to me now. This is a source of profound sorrow. We do not talk much and we don't much like each other, and that is unlikely to change. When Bill finally left our home in the fall of 2005, I tortured myself with the thought of him as an old man, with wrinkles worn into his face and white hair at his temples. I had planned on watching him get to that point. Now he will do it without me. The textures of Bill's life will be created and soothed and marked by someone else. I had not intended for that to happen.

Infidelity did not have the only hand in the decline and fall of our marriage. But if you dusted over all those years, you would find that it remains the clearest, most defined fingerprint. Left all over the house, the furniture, the dogs, the dishes, all of our friends, and our children, too, those fingerprints are detectable on every surface. They are the minutiae of our betrayal, writ small and large across nearly every year of our marriage.

THE TAO OF INFIDELITY

O IF YOU were cheating on him, why were you so upset when he cheated on you?" This from Cheryl, the friend who cuts my hair. A simple question asked out of something equally simple—curiosity, puzzlement, a desire to understand. A rational question for an irrational pursuit. For Cheryl, it was all about making sense of a reaction that seemed to make no sense at all.

One of the problems with explaining adultery is that so many conflicting things about it are true at the same time. You can commit it and still be blindsided with sadness when it is committed against you. You can love doing it and you can hate having it done to you. You can sleep with someone else, but when your spouse does the same thing it will slay you as if you were the truest soul alive. You can cheat and you can believe that you will not be cheated on.

Cheryl's question was fair. But as I experienced adultery, hers was a comparison of the rational and the irrational. Apples and oranges. Mathematics and literature. The practicality of a weather algorithm and the violence of a typhoon that drowns three thousand people. The two can go just so far in explaining each other and then you have to throw up your hands.

I could only answer her question disappointingly—I was crushed because it felt lousy. Having an affair doesn't inoculate you against the effects of one. Adultery is not a SARS vaccine. In fact, in my case having an affair likely made the discovery of one much worse.

But Cheryl has a point, even if it's an unintended one. There is a side to the whole issue that is firmly grounded in rational conduct. There is a general mind-set of logic, a Tao, to infidelity. I made use of it by squeezing that logic like a cheese to fit my purpose. Which I guess is a logic of its own. It is the lopsided, self-orbiting logic of a child: I will justify only what I am doing. It is useful only insofar as it advances my agenda.

There are so few ways to talk about adultery except in preemptive strikes of judgment and wrath. The very word fires up the kiln and burns off the oxygen around it at such an astonishing rate that breathlessness decides the moment. Someone who cheats is horrible, and disgust ensues. Someone who is cheated upon is a victim and pulls all sympathy. And that is the end of it. Quick and dirty, as if there is nothing else to discuss.

Politics provides the most accessible and comfortably distant example of how we adjudicate betrayal culturally. Some senator cheats and is found out, and word leaches through the media onto a national platform. There follows a slight shuffle among congressional peers as they back away from the betrayer, slowly, so as not to appear too callous and turncoat. But the wolves have begun to howl. An animal will soon be bleeding in the snow. Disgust is rampant. Even I am disgusted. Even the cheater is disgusted and usually says so if he wants any hope of resurrecting his future as a lobbyist or a news anchor. Eventually he resigns and the matter drifts into obscurity. After a reasonable amount of time, the adulterer reemerges as a Sunday morning talking head.

The problem with this dispatch, with wading in no deeper

than your ankles, is that you never really get anywhere. Perhaps people think there is no need. Infidelity is firmly attached to the sin and damnation side of the table of elements, and no one wants to go over there for a closer look. But simple condemnation does nothing to advance an understanding of why it happens or what drives the people doing it, or even how they accomplish it. The condemnation is a way for someone outside the blast radius to render an opinion and then, once suitably cleansed, drive home to his own intact family trailing clouds of sanctimony.

As for the person who has cheated or the person who was cheated upon, these sentiments don't provide wisdom where it is sorely needed. They are about as useful as throwing spring onions at a charging wolf. It is this way with most of the ugly issues in our lives. There is such ambivalence to wrestle meaningfully with the larger beasts until they are at the door.

Early in my marriage Bill and I were at a wedding, sitting at our table among friends during the reception. I had been a reporter at that newspaper in Princeton for about five years by then but had recently left the job to work from home, advancing a freelance practice to see whether I could make enough money doing it. I announced this to the wedding table. Our college friend Beth, never one to mince words, turned toward me in full view of the table and said, "So what do you do with that extra time, have affairs?"

What kind of provocateur asks such a question so loudly and in such company, and at a wedding? I wanted to slap her. The audacity. But of course the audacity was largely mine. I was really angry because she was right. I had been having affairs. And I was scared she had called everyone's gaze down upon me. Like a figure standing over my prone form frantically waving her hands. Hey! Look!

Over here! She had asked with a genuine if vaguely arch curiosity about adultery, and she had hit a bull's-eye.

The way Cheryl and Beth asked about adultery with such a quiet perplexity says something about the way we perceive it: that along with everything else, there must be a clean, direct logic behind its motivations. Or at least an understanding of the equation "If this happens, then this will be the result . . ." That may be true of other people. I was content to push that equation out of my frame of reference. But as for logic, yes, I applied that like a magic balm. There is much to say about the misery and the emotion surrounding an affair. But it's also true that just conducting one requires a sinister practicality. So here's an anatomy lesson in the average day and week of someone pulling this off.

By late 1990, three years after I married Bill, I had already had an affair with Tommy and an affair with Steven. During those affairs, I spent every day hungering for something I should not have had and every day plotting ways to get it. That is the general approach. It almost became a second job. I would wake up and be instantly aware that my life was way off-kilter and that my desires were misaligned with my realities. Lethargy would descend. But I'd get over it quickly because there was work to do, and I became very focused at doing it.

To put it into a single, rational word, the absolute practice of adultery always came down to one thing: want. I wanted. Infidelity with excuse and emotion and guilt and everything else cut away is simply about want. What you want may be injurious, but the *fact* of want overpowers. It goes straight to the head of the class. It bypasses all other checks and balances. When something is that fundamental, it is possible to get really rational about it, to separate the guilt from the logistics and just go after the prize. I related to every day like this, as fraught with opportunity.

The whole purpose of logic lay in using it not to get caught. If you are having an affair as a way to get out of a marriage, then be as flagrant as possible. You will have no need of logic. You will just have to wait a little while and you'll be excused from your marital obligations. But I wanted to keep from getting caught. And I wanted to have my affair. As logic can cut both ways, I edited out the parts of it that told me, Don't do this. But I retained in full working order those parts that told me, Do. Thus, logic in the extreme, shading into cunning, shading into an almost predatory forethought.

My first goal was always to shake off other people so that I could pace through the list of the seven deadly sins—lust, acedia, deceit, greed—with no one to mark my progress or get in the way. An affair needs a lot of privacy. When the lover was in my hometown, as with Tommy, it was in some ways easier, but only in some ways. The border was porous but the situation more dangerous. I could indulge my desire to see him, but I had to be more careful. There were neighbors and friends and co-workers to run into. There were patterns of movement and behavior to observe, and the details of a rendezvous had to be woven into those. There were people who knew me and who might whisper things. And there was the possibility of running into Bill at any moment.

Cell phones were not much in use back then, and Bill's whereabouts were often in question. So another goal of the day was to try to continually place him. I needed to mark down Bill's location on some mental map. It helped me to create alibis and manipulate schedules. I would say to myself, I know he's at work in Manhattan right now and that even if he left this very moment and sped home,

I will still have about two hours before I could possibly be caught. Therefore I can get to Tommy's apartment, hang out for a good hour, and still get home in time to recover my married posture. This factoring of time and chance became a daily habit. I would set my days to it and my nights as well.

I wrapped work responsibilities around it, careful that everything got finished. But finished in a way that preserved my time with Tommy.

I manufactured excuses for every evening that I was out with him. But they had to reflect enough of the truth that I could remember them later.

I staged arguments with Bill so that I could storm out of the house in a pretend fury and so get myself time away from the marriage with justification. And then I would go immediately to Tommy's apartment.

I was careful about what I said and careful discussing where I had been during the day. I could not suddenly talk about having been up in Milford, New Jersey, for lunch when Bill knew I had never previously been to Milford, New Jersey, for lunch.

I asked a friend to take down and keep hidden my lover's name and number and information, so that she could get hold of him in case something dire happened to me.

I thought ahead in every conversation I had with Bill, steering its drift into safer paths. My thoughts jumped urgently in front of my words, nasty little hyenas scavenging for the possibility of danger, the threat of discovery.

I had male friends and I worked that angle often in case someone said to Bill, I saw your wife today in town with some guy. I could answer that I was getting lunch with my colleague Daveed. Or my high school friend Robert. Or my other colleague Petey.

I was very obvious about being in the company of safe, known men who would be familiar to Bill. Friends of the opposite sex were permissible in our marriage, for him and for me. He had them, I had them. I leaned often on this license during my affairs because I wanted to make being out in public with someone I was not married to an unremarkable occurrence.

But being in bed with Tommy was a different matter. It usually took the most energy of all and a serious manipulation of the facts to get there. I needed to get to Tommy's apartment, with or without an invitation, and I needed to know ahead of time if he would be around. Otherwise there would be a missed opportunity. Time with him was precious and bought with a high cost to personal sanity. I didn't want to waste a lie on nothing.

The difficulty ratcheted up when the relationship was with a man from out of town. The affair with Steven was conducted off-soil, in South Carolina, far away from my home. Although the separation intensified my longing to see him, it also laid down a barrier of impenetrability. It threw up a wall that permitted me to go right up to but not beyond.

This made it easier to deny myself, a discipline that never came to me easily. I learned to tell myself, No, that you cannot do. You cannot drive down to South Carolina overnight, miss six days of work, and explain it all away. You cannot buy airline tickets and disappear for twenty-four hours. You cannot call his house. Ever. Logic would kick in to thwart that possibility before it even got tempting. I was an über-rationalist at drawing a line in my own sand if something was just outside the neighborhood of reason.

Bill's business travel made it easier. I became very good at the art of casting ahead to the hours and nights that would be available to me. If Bill was leaving for a day or two, I would fill those hours with adultery. I would make my schedule conform to them whether it was a work schedule, a hotel schedule, a flight, or a meal. I fulfilled all the responsibilities of work and home, but the hours of fulfilling them were shoved around according to need. I exerted a lot of muscle rearranging things.

A few months after I met Steven, we were trying to work out how to see each other again. By that point we had been together for only five days and were not anywhere near sated. There were 740 miles of federal highway between us. It was not to be an easy logistic. I remember my relief, then, when Bill called me at home one afternoon to say he'd be leaving for Russia again in two days and did I know where his passport was.

As soon as I found the passport—every detail had to be assured first—I got in touch with Steven. We had just a few days of planning, and the decisions were necessarily urgent. This Russian trip was what we had. It might be all we had. I did not have children yet, so I was still relatively mobile. But I never wanted to do anything too unusual or inexplicable or too odd. I had just been down in South Carolina. It would have been oddness itself to go back down there so abruptly. Steven would have to come up to New Jersey, where I worked. And so he did. He took the train from South Carolina, up to Princeton and stayed with me there for three days. I picked him up at the train station and we had one of those romantic platform reunions that make everyone around you smile wistfully.

It was wonderful to be with him again. But it all had to be tempered with a strict, calibrated logic. So I took a day off from my job, but not two. I made hotel reservations for him, but not too close to home. I stayed there with him until late at night, but I did not stay all night. I let two close friends know what I was doing, but I didn't expose them to an encounter. Always there was an envelope whose edge had to be pushed but not fallen over. I became very calculated. I measured every risk and took them all up to a point. Logic kicked into high gear, keen to every possibility and supernaturally alert to danger. I functioned with a vigilance largely unavailable to me— because unnecessary—during normal married life.

Strangely, none of this caused me to question why I was having an affair. The stress was part of the landscape of deceit, and I knew that. If I was going to cheat, then I was going to have to know how it really felt. I imagined the feelings I had for Steven and the pleasure of our relationship would offset the stress of hiding his presence in my life, of squeezing it into the narrowest seam. The balance came close but usually tipped toward the side of allure. As long as it did, I stayed right where I was.

Months later, there was another possibility necessitating some last-minute, jury-rigged plans. I was missing Steven terribly. I needed a rendezvous, but they did not come easily. So I drummed up an idea to do a story on bonefishing the flats off of Islamorada, down in the Florida Keys. The story was a ruse. I wanted to get away with Steven such that we would be not just away in South Carolina but away in Florida. We were both married, and he lived at the bottom of the country. The situation demanded an extraordinary alibi. So I set about working one up.

The story would serve as an excuse to get me away from Bill

and into Steven's orbit, alone. We wanted to be where no one knew us, where we could walk around and go fishing and sit at a bar and buy beer at a local market just as if we were a real couple, with nothing to hide. I remember querying a magazine editor, my head spinning from the task of explaining why this story made sense, why it was such a good idea, and how I would do it. I importuned her with an almost frantic sense of persuasion. She must have thought I was a very intense reporter. Well, I was. But there were two reasons for my intensity, and the story was only one of them.

Once the assignment was secure, I called Steven. I had married my desire to see him with the alibi, and I was off. I do not think anything would have stopped me at the time. Logic. Necessity. Jury-rigging. There was a motive behind every action.

I learned how to do new things because this was a way to be with these men openly. It lent some legitimacy to my conduct, I told myself. So I learned how to drive a boat. I learned how to cast a light tackle rod. I learned about bonefish. I learned better how to drink and hang out at the pub in town. These were not just hobbies to fill up the hours when I wasn't having sex. These gave me a way to talk about the affairs without admitting to them. If I could talk about boating or fishing or hunting, then I was bringing with subversive acuity the details of my days and nights into my legitimate world.

This was not done to mock my relationship with Bill or to make a fool of him. This was done to turn down some of the pressure. Though it was a world away from the truth, there was enough truth in it that it provided some level of release. I diced up the stress to make it less onerous. I told myself, It's not the whole truth, but it is some of the truth. I really was out drinking with friends tonight. I really was boating. I really was doing a story down in the Keys. And it would have to be enough. That is how I lived with myself. I used logic to help me divide it all into manageable compartments so that I rarely had to look at my duplicity full on.

Oh yes, logic has a place in infidelity. It is the manic, burned-down logic of a fugitive. When it forms the basis of each day, it becomes second nature. You can bend every responsibility to its purpose, and so I did. If I needed to work, I would visit Tommy during lunchtime or right after. If I needed to meet Bill for dinner, I would arrange a rendezvous for another night or for lunchtime the next day. If Bill was away, well, then all bets were off. I was away, too.

When you are talking about the next day or the next week of having an affair, this is a relatively easy gymnastic. It's when you begin to apply the exercise to a larger time frame—weeks ahead, months out—that rational thought decides to quit. Says, You've stretched me to the breaking point. I've had enough, I'm out of here. Raw emotion takes over finally. It makes you reckless. It threatens the whole enterprise because you're in a situation that will do nothing but get worse. Infidelity has a reverse half-life. It gets more noxious over time.

So to keep it working, you function in smaller and smaller increments. You parcel your life out into little units of now and now and now. The average human being is not good at this. Buddhists, yes. Masai warriors, yes. The rest of us are not on the same level. And that's generally where it begins to go bad. Where logic leaves off and you run on emotion, the messiest fuel there is. That is how you will get caught.

Bill must have felt exactly this way one Friday afternoon in the early summer of 1998. He came very close to blowing it for himself, although I see this only now. We had rented a beach house at the shore for the three of us—me, Bill, and our first son, then just about three years old. When Bill came home from work that Friday, I was packing. He stopped in the hallway and stared at me, wanted to know why I was packing for him. *Of course I am packing for you, why wouldn't I?* Because I'm not going with you to the shore. *What do you mean, you're not going with us to the shore?* I have to work. *Yes, but not until Monday. You could have two days down there with us.* I'm not going with you; I'm staying here this weekend. You can go down without me.

Even then it was a red flag. A father should vacation with his family. But I was impatient with acknowledging that. I had no desire to create explanations for Bill. The obvious did not occur to me because I hadn't bothered to stitch together the evidence, and everything between us otherwise seemed to be fine. I have always taken things at face value. I saw the shore problem as a matter of miscommunication. But still, I could not puzzle out why my husband would have me go down there alone with our son for the weekend when his natural place was with us. It was odd. And once you allow oddness to creep into the picture it is the deuce and all to get it out again.

Bill dug in his heels and refused to go with us. He held to his own nonsensical path. I couldn't understand it. I couldn't understand it to such a degree that I dug in heels of my own. We stayed home that weekend, all three of us, so that I unknowingly thwarted whatever secret plans Bill had made. He was forced to wait because I didn't leave until Monday. He seethed with frustration all weekend. He should have acted with less agitation. By then Bill was betraying not just me but logic itself. He made no sense. He must have been desperate to see her, though I didn't know who "her" was then or even that there was a "her." But he was running on emotion. And from that point he ought to have begun counting the days or weeks until I would find out.

Several weeks later, I found out. This was his second affair. His first was with Anne the stripper, and his own journal tucked in under a pile of shirts gave him away then. In this second affair, it was the phone bill that did him in.

They are the undoing of so many betrayals. It is an abuse of logic to overlook those details. Can you not think forward enough to cover your own tracks? Can you not conceive? If you are going to repeatedly call a place that is unusual to your spouse, you are going to get caught. There was an Atlantic City number, her number, splashed all over our phone bill. Of course I called it, because I did not know that we had any acquaintance there. It was an ill-divining name if ever there was one, even just the look of it on the printed page.

There was something else. Two years earlier, in 1996, Bill had left me and our then one-year-old son abruptly one weekend to drive down to Atlantic City. He said he just needed a little man-time to smoke a cigar, shoot some craps, be alone. This seemed reasonable. I could understand the need for a little vacation. Raising a child is labor-intensive, and a break is essential to the task. So he went with my blessing.

What was not reasonable were my repeated attempts to get hold of him that weekend. Our son had fallen into a delirium of fever. I was nervous all alone watching over such a sick child, his little limbs lethargic as I brushed him with a damp washcloth, his cheeks flushed a brilliant red as I laid my hand against them. I called Bill many times over the two days that he was in Atlantic City. The calls went unanswered until Sunday afternoon when he was driving home. And then it was less about answers than about him screaming into the phone. I had disturbed him, he told me angrily. He hadn't been able to relax because of all my phone messages. Was I crazy, he asked, making those calls when I knew where he was? I remember my astonishment. Our son was sick. Where was his father's concern? The damage was enormous. Bill arrived home to a silent house and my growing conviction that I wasn't going to have much parenting help from my mate.

I can only assume that it was all part of a simple strategy. In the argument, he had created a disturbance bound to keep me, angry as I was, off his back for a few days while he resettled into the home. And his confessed trip gave him a way to talk about the affair without mentioning it. To relieve some of the pressure. He had in fact been in Atlantic City. He had in fact needed a weekend off. There was enough truth in his own ruse that his mind converted the rest quite neatly into a plausible explanation. Minus the telling fact of whom he had been down there with.

Fast-forward to the fall of 1998 and I am dialing a number down in Atlantic City that is all over my phone bills. The space between finding that number and hearing her voice was transformative. I remember thinking, Yes. Now I know. I know what I am going to find at the other end of that call. I am going to find Her. I knew it even as I dialed. It is astonishing how long you can ignore the evidence right in front of you and then suddenly, in a moment thin as a sacrificial wafer, you know. I dialed the number and got an answering machine with a woman's name. The name Susan.

I was alone in my kitchen because my son was asleep, taking a nap upstairs. I heard the sound of another woman's voice on the answering machine. It was Susan's voice, composed and workaday, as if there were nothing in her world she needed to be wary of: "You've reached Susan. I'm not home right now, so please leave a message." I left a message all right. You know how you press an elevator button and then you hear the whoosh of hydraulics behind the door, gearing up? That was me. My hydraulics kicked in full-throttle. I became a Fury, cursing into the phone. I left a classic, cuckold-wife tirade on that machine, a storm of anger in a voice that sounded nothing like my own. I think I was channeling Lucifer, or at least Linda Blair. Both would have been proud. And then I hung up and dialed Bill's office number.

When he answered I demanded to know about Susan. Or rather, I told him that I knew and demanded to know why. I do not now remember what his reaction was then, apart from quickly getting off the phone. He came home early that afternoon and almost as abruptly left our house for several days and fell into a cycle of nonresponse. I remember only crying, and yelling, and feeling every bit as blighted as he must have felt ten years before when I told him about Tommy.

Through it all, again, I was certain of one thing. I did not want our marriage to end. I was crushed but not finished. And I told him this. Again. As I had after Anne the stripper. When he came back home days later, we began the arduous trek back toward a marriage. We were edgy and unhappy, and we didn't talk about it much because Bill did not want to. In my ignorance, though, I assumed that was the end of it. But I had a name. Not just a city this time, but a name. Another woman's name to follow Anne the stripper. The name Susan. That name will always be with me, along with the person who belongs to it. Her life has since been grafted onto my own.

Surge forward yet again several years to Thanksgiving in 2004, another night when logical behavior was defied and brought discovery in its wake. The fight-and-flight thing—where you stage a fit and then leave in theatrical disgust to gain yourself some time off from the marriage—had been in use far too frequently by Bill over the months leading up to that November. The pattern was obvious to everyone. My mother was skeptical about whether Bill would show up for dinner. She thought he would cut out beforehand in a storm of rage. He was constantly erupting and leaving, erupting and leaving. It is no wonder, considering that by then he was hiding not only a mistress but a newborn child. I told my mother I was determined not to let an argument ruin a holiday again, and I became the very personification of calm.

That afternoon, it began. Bill squirmed and argued his way through the lead-up, trying to rope me in, trying to create a diversionary storm. I remained passive. I just wanted to have a nice Thanksgiving with all of us together. Since that failed to secure a fair exit, Bill suddenly said he didn't want to go with us to Thanksgiving dinner. He suddenly wanted to drive up to White Plains, New York, where his own family was celebrating. He said he would go there alone. He tore upstairs in frustration. He must have felt utterly trapped. After much pleading, I finally got him to agree that we would go to my parents' home, but he wanted to drive separately. They lived about three miles away. His behavior was absurd. And more than that, illogical.

Immediately upon arriving at my parents' home, Bill announced that he had to leave. He said he needed to go home and get his book. The one he was reading. The book he was engrossed in. We all stood amazed. Why was there such a need to get a book? You don't read through Thanksgiving dinner. He was steadfast. Even when I offered to drive home and get his book for him. I remember his very manner, stiff and affected. He wouldn't look at me but averted his eyes like a bad dog as he slunk out the door.

He did finally return about ninety minutes later. He carried through the door a book he never touched again through the evening. He even forgot it at my parents' home at the end of the holiday dinner. My mother called me the following morning. "Bill forgot his book that he was so anxious to get last night," she said in a too-even tone.

I am afraid my whole family was suspicious from then on, particularly my mother, who narrowed her figurative gaze at him. When she called the next morning, she asked if things had settled down. Of course they had, I told her. Bill had left early, off on some ill-defined sequence of errands. That was the first time she asked me, Where does Bill go on all those nights he leaves the house? I think you should try, she told me, to insist that Bill do more with you and the boys, as a family.

But again, it was about three months after Thanksgiving, in January 2005, just after the Beslan hostage crisis in Russia, that I found out. About Her. About the house nearby. About the baby. Shocked to the point of awe, I remember thinking back to these two scenarios that had played out so unsatisfactorily: Susan in Atlantic City and the Thanksgiving book episode. These were among the first pieces of a much larger matrix I would scroll through in the coming months. Neither of those earlier scenarios had jibed with logic. Logic will carry you only as long as you are devoted to it. It is the one thing you cannot betray.

It wasn't until later that afternoon of finding out that it occurred to me to ask who the woman was. What her name was. I had already been told about her and about the baby. I had already made that phone call to Bill's other office in Mississippi. People had already gathered at my house. I don't know why this single fact took so long to reveal itself, but it's easy to see how it could be lost in the chaos. I remember turning to one of my friends and asking, What is the name of Bill's mistress?

Her name, of course, was Susan.

Susan from Atlantic City. Susan from the phone bills. Susan from the Thanksgiving book night. Susan had been trailing alongside us all those years. Their affair had been fully in place through summers and winters and first days of school and shore trips and late night dinners and the sex I shared with my husband. She had been there straight through the birth of our second son. She had been around since eight months after the birth of our first son. Ten years already. One decade. In a shadow marriage with my husband. It was a day of shock upon shock upon shock.

Logic as I knew it and had practiced it blinkered out, a thin line of white light on the screen condensing down to nothing. I felt vacuumed over, and a white noise washed my ears of every other sound. I was in for a strange new world, governed by emotion and tumult and reaction and a strange cottony overlay of shock.

I was good at compartmentalization. But Bill must have been a master at it. Competence at a level that might be recognizable to people who commit massive public frauds and nevertheless manage to function well right up to the edge of discovery. I have tried to ask him over the years how he did this. How he kept it all so neatly divided, me and her and our sons and their pregnancy and their baby and our home and their house, for ten full years. In this way I am not unlike my friend Cheryl and our friend Beth—part of you wants to shove aside all the emotion and just ask out of basic curiosity, How? Part of you just wants to hear the daily play of detail, of maneuver, of how so much was kept hidden for so long. Of how he did it. Of what it did to him.

I never got anywhere. During the ten months in 2005 after the discovery of his affair with Susan—from the day I found out until the day he left home for good—Bill answered almost no questions about it. My information, sketchy to this day, came mostly from other people. Except in minute bits of grief and explanation, Bill refused to talk with me about the reality of their long affair. He would just go silent, or leave the room, or leave the house, or hang up the phone, or take a shower, or refuse to call back, or develop a sudden urge to clean the cellar, or yell, or disappear, or run an errand, or hide his phone, or threaten—anything, anything to keep from answering my questions. It has remained this way right up to the present.

This is not my way. I explain everything, even if my explanations make little sense to anyone else. Explanation is a powerful seducer. We use it to keep uncertainties at a distance. It is usually imposed upon whatever weird truth we're trying to explain away, bent and squeezed and even tortured to fit some round truth that the square conduct confounds. The fact is that explanation helps.

Bill wouldn't give me one. But I still needed to understand how he managed the whole thing. In its absence I had to come up with my own explanation for him. I would use it to frame out a way to think about his grand-scale deceit. Not to compare it with my own affairs as a basis for condemnation. Just to understand how he did it. And although the frame I came up with is a simple, almost charming metaphor for his betrayal, it is nevertheless the one I use. Carl Linnaeus—the Swedish botanist, the father of taxonomy, the father of a universal classification of plants and mosses and lichens, the father of naming things—gave a name to Bill's modus operandi.

At his home in Uppsala, Sweden, Linnaeus kept a garden maintained through Uppsala University, where he was a professor of medicine. He tended the herb beds and medicinal plants. He established his own order there so that his students, bent over the garden, could take pattern and meaning away from the chaotic sprawl of botany. Linnaeus divided things up. He organized the garden into a system of "parterres," or compartments. He had a perennial parterre and an annual parterre, a cold frame and a southern parterre. This compartmentalization was so thorough and so useful that it exists there today, and you can see it if you go.

Its usefulness expands into metaphor. It is how I think about Bill's affair and his life with Susan and their baby. There was the wife parterre and the parterre for our sons. There was the parterre for the mistress and one—larger, weedier, harder to prune into submission—for the baby. He tended them individually, although some more diligently than others. Some he outright neglected, let go wild and speculative. Some he gave a stronger devotion. But everything along the way was divided up.

I picture him stepping gingerly between the borders. I do not know if the transitions caused him pain or brought on the torment that attends any double life. But I can imagine him thinking, Now it's time to manage this parterre and leave off with the others. Now I have to go over here. Now I'd better pause over this one for a moment, as I've let it go too long. He could function within each separation as if that were the only parterre of the moment. This, I imagine, is how he kept his mental footing. Through a relentless compartmentalization of reality. It is a testimony to the power of logic, of rationality, of order imposed where there isn't any, or shouldn't be.

HEADWATERS

MY FAMILY HAS always had a hearty alliance with guns. Guns played a big role in the cascade of genetic hand-me-downs I got from my prickly forebears. Along with impatience and a tendency to roar at people who do not necessarily deserve it, I received the gift of aim.

My grandmother was a fierce competitor on the East Coast trapshooting circuit and a gunwoman her entire life. I have a photograph of her standing at a match wearing her shooting vest, cradling a shotgun, her grandmotherly, spun-sugar crown of white hair confounding the whole image. My aunt was on several state championship trapshooting teams. And my uncle went hunting nearly every year in castle parks in Scotland, where he drank a lot of whiskey and shot a lot of pheasants.

But my father was the biggest gunman in my life. When I was growing up, there was a stuffed Kodiak bear in our house he had shot in Alaska. An overzealous taxidermist mounted it on a rock with one paw raised and its mouth open, fangs bared. It was the biggest thing in our recreation room. There were heads everywhere in there—mule deer, antelope, caribou, elk, and a few Pennsylvania whitetail. I used to decorate their antlers.

My father is a member of a local hunting club that still has its base in a stately Georgian-style home on the banks of the Delaware

River. The men I met there as an adolescent contributed to my impression of how adult men act. They wore tweed jackets and gun vests and drank expensive whiskey and played serious poker, but not loudly. They were old-school, wealthy gentlemen and eccentric as ibex, every last one of them. In their company I learned how to shoot pigeons. I didn't much like it. It seemed mean and stupid and kind of pointless. But I liked being with my father and I loved being around all those sporting men.

I wonder if this helps to explain Terry. Terry appeared on the scene in the spring of 1991. I wonder if that is why I felt such an instant attraction to his kind of man. Terry hunted. Terry was comfortable around guns. One looks for any excuse.

I knew Terry from my school district, but only marginally, as he was five years younger than me. Our families crossed paths in our hometown but I hadn't seen him since we were in elementary school. I ran into Terry one afternoon at a local delicatessen and couldn't talk for blushing. My, he had grown. He looked Nordic. His cheekbones were wide as a wingspan and his eyes as blue as an acetylene torch. I stammered my way through a polite conversation about our respective families, keenly aware of an increasingly ungovernable attraction until we hit on the topic of the National Rifle Association. At which point I found my voice and lost my blush. We argued for the next half an hour. Which is a good way to begin, I think.

Two days later, I was walking my dog along a canal near that deli. There were thirty miles of river canal within a short distance of my home, tracing a line from my hometown all the way up to Upper Ediston and beyond. I could have stomped along any of them. I chose, instead, the mile or so that encompasses the deli. I chose it on purpose because I was out looking for Terry. But he found me on the canal. So he was out looking, too.

Terry was my third affair. The affair lasted through the spring and summer months of 1991, utterly supplanting my relationship with Bill. It was an outdoor adventure from start to stop. At the time, Terry lived up the road from my parents' home, where they had twelve acres of woodland and pasture. I think that property more than anything seduced Terry into my life. We used it well, both for hunting and for hiding in it. He once told me he had never made love to a woman wearing camo gear.

With Terry, I learned archery. That is where the family aim came in. I was good at it. I loved the tight tension on my compound bow such that the more I went to full draw, the stronger my arms got. The more I practiced, the more easily I could hit the center of a target from a tree stand twenty yards away. The more I nocked arrows, the more quickly I could nock arrows. Terry would steady my bow by wrapping his arm all the way around my body when he could just as easily have done it from the near side.

His was the only affair that smacked of hearth and gun, taxidermy and buckshot. It felt like coming home. I am sure that Terry would have been the kind of son-in-law my father would have preferred. They could have gone out every weekend and blasted geese out of the sky together. My affair with Terry cast into form the pull of men and guns that I had been exposed to since my childhood. That was its initial hold on me. That, and the drama of a new romance. Always the drama. I can't remember a time when I wasn't out looking for that, too.

I was born on the windy side of the personality island. The leeward side bores me. If it's blowing a gale of emotion, that is where

I want to be. I can burn along on a Mach 10 dramatic rip as easily as I can lie on the couch. This is probably owing to the way I was raised and the family I was raised in. When I look for the earliest seeds of my erratic marital behavior, this is where I start.

My family, bless them all, should not be allowed out in public. My father drives like a Valkyrie, curses in front of strangers, and used to disappear for several weeks a year in pursuit of elk and caribou and mule deer. My sister can argue from zero to sixty in a matter of seconds. My brother is a master wedge, dividing even the calmest person from his equanimity. My mother has experienced every neurosis known to humankind, most of them simultaneously. And I, being the middle child, am the sum total of all of it. Our family crest should have a cumulonimbus cloud on it.

An average Plump family Christmas reveals us at our contentious best. We are WASPs for whom appearance is religion, so the spread itself is perfect. The food, the place settings, the crystal candleholders, the tablecloth like a layer of glistening snow. However, once the prayers are intoned we argue about everything, and we do it loudly. It's gladiatorial. It ends with people shaking in fury or on the verge of mental collapse. We love to argue. It's in our blood. Both sets of grandparents yelled like harpies, and every child, grandchild, and cousin has been armed to the teeth with this trait. The calmer family members have all but died out. Darwin smiles.

Last Christmas, the younger set opened fire on my uncle, a retired navy captain who allowed that women in the military are a scourge. The lovely table set by my sister divided like Korea without the demilitarized zone. A few in-laws cannot deal with this, and they almost always leave the table, gasping for air. The rest of us stay until the bitter end, feeding off mysterious reserves of energy. We manifested the most combative Christmas in history excepting that one on the Delaware River involving some Hessians. That historical site in Washington Crossing, by the way, is not far from our childhood home. I do not think this is a coincidence.

We cry when the news is good, when it's bad, and when it's indecipherable. We argue about nothing, and when that peters out we argue about the other side of nothing. We wreck appliances that annoy us. We bang things on tables, like Khrushchev. We could field a rugby team at a moment's notice. A more provocative, emotional, argumentative, shrubbery- and appliance-wrecking family cannot be imagined. Still, it's how we do things. Growing up, I considered the formula largely successful in nurturing a nuclear family. It did, however, have an influence on my practice of relationships, which were rarely worthy unless they could pitch up to a squall.

There were other factors, though, each of them stirring up and muddying the declarative equation of my upbringing. My first real boyfriend in high school, Tim, ruined me for romance because he was so good to me. He was supernaturally good. His love served as a litmus test for every other man who came along after. At the age of seventeen, Tim was both passionate and loving and so much fun. We learned everything together in the back of his black VW Bug with the radio on full-bore. Just hearing a song off of *Born to Run* is enough to summon him completely.

But Tim also had the necessary component of crazy that kept it all interesting. I recall going to one of his ice hockey games in high school where I watched him thrash past three teammates in an attempt to get at his opponent. I was impressed. I was intrigued. I thought, Yep, he's for me. Tim was the best introduction to romantic love that a young woman could wish for. He set a precariously high standard. I have found its like only once since then.

Tim also introduced me to the concept of monogamy, in which you love one person a whole lot for a very, very long time. My appreciation of it lasted a year and a half, until I went off to college. It would be a while before I could string together that many months of fidelity. Once in a relationship of any length, I had to charge it up, do something to get the dramatic fix of those first flush months of passion. Adhering to one man was not one of them.

This would seem to lead irrevocably to a life of high drama. And it has. I was raised on it, and I have picked up the tattered standard and brandished it throughout my decades. There were familial experiences that contributed to my tendency to seek it out. But the path is never so straightforward and explicable. I could throw in the complication of my parents, whose relationship does nothing to demystify my own.

They have a good and even marriage. After fifty-five years they are still devoted. They hold hands. My father dotes and is very protective. My mother irons his clothes and picks out his favorite foods. They are rarely without each other. I am amazed at their adoration. They grouse more now than they used to, but the love sings on. A child is an adept observer of the parental relationship. Even if there are problems that do not show up outright, rancor is obvious and so is disdain. I never saw either when I was growing up. Not once. My family was everywhere else combative, but my parents were a harbor of quiet boats where their marriage was concerned. Just for a romantic lark, I helped my mother haul out her wedding dress in celebration of their fortieth anniversary. She walked down the long hall of our home in it, my father called out from the living room for the surprise. He took one look at her and wept like a sailor coming home as he walked down the hallway to enfold her in his arms.

People tell me this is not proof of fidelity or even of a successful marriage, about which I think they're crazy. I would stake my life on my parents' fidelity. They were just those sorts of people. My father liked to hunt and fish and smoke three packs ("One pack!") of Marlboros a day. He ran a lumberyard. He cursed. Lots. He is a man's man. That is the world he inhabits. Based on my perspective of him, man's men do not cheat. They get jazzed just by being manly.

And then there is my mother. When I was a cantankerous adolescent, I used to complain that her life would draw the wrath of the gods. She was too cocooned in the luxury of money and safety and a good marriage, not challenged enough by life. I thought she was cavalier about her luck, like every other WASP I knew. She is reserved and ladylike and lucky as hell. Either that or she had all the fight sucked out of her by her own contentious family of origin.

I mention my parents because it seems that their example would have put me on the road to a wholesome marriage. That is what the experts claim, anyway. I had a solid, loving model right before my eyes. But for some reason it didn't take. I couldn't have interpreted it any messier than I did. Their steadfastness, regardless of what these experts might say of the necessity of a good example, didn't do anything for me. This is both vexing and relieving: vexing because you would want the fidelity lesson to repeat; relieving because I can tell myself that the poor example Bill and I have set won't necessarily trickle down through our sons.

Then there was Bill's family. He hailed from an Irish Catholic family in White Plains straight out of Central Casting. His mother held three jobs during their childhood to augment coffers severely strained by lots of private Catholic schooling. She was an eccentric. She dried clothes in the oven. She dressed like a carpenter. She went to church about fifty times a week. She gathered her own wood (probably split it, too). She talked a blue streak and called me "Wen." I don't think I ever saw her sit down to dinner. Everything she cooked turned brown, even and especially the broccoli. It was obvious from the first moment I met her how much she adored her sons. I would never come up to speed in her eyes.

Bill's father, Ted, was kind, very intellectual, and very smart. But Bill always said theirs was not a particularly happy union. I think Ted was forced into an aloof posture by the strain of his marriage. And why shouldn't it have been strained—they had six children in nearly that many years with hardly the means to support them. But Ted was a good father, a focused provider, a man who loved his children. Bill always said this, too. He said Ted never missed a track meet or a football game or a child's performance, and he said it with admiration and warmth. I don't think Bill faulted his parents for their flawed marriage. I think he noted it and then accepted it, which I always thought was a very decent thing for him to do.

Apart from his role as a father, Ted was wonderful to sit and talk with. He loved the roll and pitch and yawl of words. Once when I went up to visit Bill in White Plains before we were married, Ted gave me a list of collective nouns for birds just because he thought I would like it. Prior to that, I thought "flock of birds" was a mere descriptor. It was not. It was part of a specific lexicon for common birds that, even though they are common, rings with poetry: a sedge of bitterns, a charm of finches, a parliament of owls, a lamentation of swans.

Bill's father wrote two books on sports. I have copies of them on my shelves, though why I should still have them is beyond me. They hold testimony to the myriad ways people express their love, even when that expression is difficult. The first book, about the greatest U.S. athletes of the twentieth century, was inscribed thus to Bill on the inside cover: "Bill: All the best, Ted." I am not sure there is a better illustration of how understated Bill's examples were. But the second book, about the greatest athletes of Europe, was published a few months before Ted's death from cancer. It was inscribed: "Billy, I love you, Dad."

Despite their lack of money, Bill's parents managed to put six children through good colleges. Notre Dame. Lehigh. Duke. MIT. Bill's brothers and sisters were all bright and funny and deeply sarcastic. If they picked on you, they liked you. If you were ignored, you might as well never darken their doorstep again. But the example of fidelity rested there, too. Of the seven marriages in Bill's family, only two, including ours, have gone down in flames. The others, though sorely tested by fate, look to have the very mark of longevity.

Bill and I were to have an Episcopal wedding, but with a Catholic priest, one of his family friends, also in attendance on the altar. He conducted the Pre-Cana session for Bill and me the month before our wedding. That was held at the shore home of an infamous trucking magnate because the priest happened to be vacationing there. Someone had recently tried to blow up the trucking magnate and very nearly succeeded. I was alarmed to be in his house, partly because I'd never met so obvious a mobster before and partly because I don't like explosions going off in my vicinity. So although I loved the brief, intriguing questions about marriage being thrown out to us, the session's air of sanctity was somewhat compromised. I kept shifting in my seat. I kept wondering where the mobster was. If he was going out to his car, for example, or reaching for something in his closet or wearing a flak jacket. The Mafia has its own code of fidelity, but I do not think marriage much enters into it.

I assume Bill approached the altar with every intention of doing the right thing. Don't we all? I'm not sure that I did. Even as I took my vows, I was aware of some mocking little voice in my head, particularly when I got to that part about forsaking all others. I spoke those lines as required. My entire acquaintance was in the audience—I would have read through the whole Pentateuch aloud if that had been asked of me in that magnificent cathedral with those witnesses in attendance. But a voice in my head pitched a mocking fit when I uttered that vow. It said, *Oh, really? You do, do you? You plan to forsake all others? You plan to forsake any others?*

I have thought about this nasty mental soliloquy a lot. Not as justification. I do not mean to say that I was aware of my duplicity so therefore it's excusable. What I mean is that I wondered at myself as I walked down the aisle. I loved Bill and I wanted to marry him. There were no doubts on that. Why, then, did some part of my awareness jeer at me from the pews, mocking my resolve as if I knew very well that adultery had already taken root in me?

I felt utterly galvanized in other ways. I did mean that vow about being together until death. To me that was the most important. That one said, I will love you and stay with you and keep you company through every tempest until we die. To this day, fidelity to the largest cause is one of my main motivations, even if I split the ones beneath it like kindling. I may have strayed. I would never have left.

I think what I took that day was less a complete vow than a

compass vow—a vow in a specific direction. Due west. Toward longevity. I would be true to all the promises that fell in the western quadrant—see you through sickness, stay with you in financial ruin, hold your hand as you take your last breath. This may be my only expression of fidelity. I wonder where I might have found some better models of how to conduct myself.

As a young woman, I schooled my romantic sensibilities on the most impossible examples, through classic novels and plays and poetry keening with reckless love. *Romeo and Juliet* is one of my favorites, but it has had a ridiculous impact. Right up there with my first high school love, Tim, it threw off my romantic equilibrium. The language makes me drunk. The plot distorts my sense of relationship. The ending throws off my expectation for all endings. I once plotted out the length of time it took Romeo and Juliet to conjoin. This is the kind of thing that occupies my mind. Romeo and Juliet meet on a Sunday night at the Capulets' party, are married Monday afternoon, part Tuesday morning after a night of consummation, and are both dead by Thursday. Before daybreak.

Four days. Four days for one of the world's greatest stories of love and marriage to play out. I don't know how that is an example for the rest of us. If every marriage on record lasted only four days from the first breathless encounter to a mere ninety-six hours after, then there wouldn't even be a word for infidelity. There wouldn't be a word for divorce. There wouldn't be time for anything but sex and adoration. Sounds like a charming recipe. I just have trouble practicing it in extension.

Perhaps it's unfair to use art and literature as models for anything apart from what the genius of the human mind can encompass. But I don't know what recourse we have when so many examples around us are inadequate to our needs. No one actually wants to follow the bad examples, yet even the good ones—as my own life illustrates—do not necessarily quicken within us.

Marriage equates with normal for me. Divorce among my parents' generation and their friends and acquaintances was rare and is still highly disreputable. I had aunts and uncles who were married. Grandparents, married. Friends' parents, teachers, neighbors, ministers, and pharmacists, married. It was a smallish town I grew up in, and the values of the old country prevailed even into the 1960s and 1970s. Divorce was unusual. Adultery? I imagine that was a different matter.

I first came smack up against adultery as a young woman far from home, in Italy. A girlfriend and I were fresh off a semester studying at Oxford University in England, and I was still high on its atmosphere. To be in that ancient university town, to take classes and hear lectures with those brilliant dons exhorting us in their cutglass English accents, was a seminal experience. I recall waking up on one of the few early mornings when I was not hung over and leaning out of my window to look at the gargoyles crowning the buildings around me, crouching in the half-light. It was very calm and very quiet, and the horizon was roseate. I remember thinking, Yes. This is exactly where I should be.

After Oxford, I traveled the rest of Europe for the summer with one of the women I'd met in the program. Tracy and I went to Italy first to stay with friends of my parents. Tracy and I were magnificently hosted—taken on picnics at vineyards, walked through cobbled villages, toured through alpine meadows. All went well until I was awakened in the middle of the night by one of the family's sons telling me to get Tracy out of the house. Apparently Tracy had been caught sleeping with his father. His father? He was old, for God's sake, he was in his early fifties. Tracy was twenty. Yuck. Even after coming fully awake I couldn't grasp it. They were having sex? While his wife slept upstairs?

I think my reflexes were a little slow because I was pissed off at the son. Looking back, I am embarrassed by this. I don't know what I expected the poor boy to do. Not interrupt our vacation, I suppose. I barely even knew adultery was a sin back then. I had been a virgin within a few meager years of that episode, and the creed and obligation of monogamous sex was still a bit murky. We did indeed leave the house the next morning, covered in shame.

That was my first contact with adultery, and I was unmoved by its torments. Tracy and I left before the real fallout. We didn't have to confront the wife. We moved on to France and hardly gave the incident another thought. My response, my underwhelm at the son's anguish, my annoyance at being removed from our nest of comfort, is another sign of how the whole idea of fidelity hadn't quite gelled for me. Now, of course, I can see it plainly.

An affair that intrudes into the home is more destructive, I think, than one that happens only off home turf. My affairs were conducted off premises in another house or another state. There were no near misses at the house I shared with Bill. No men slipping frantically out the upstairs window while Bill came in through the front door. No unexplained phone calls in the middle of the night. About the closest I ever came to getting caught in the act was just after I had kissed Tommy good-bye in a parking lot outside the bar in Brandywine where we had been drinking. I passed Bill on the road going home as he was driving out to look for me. We both pulled over. I was breathless with excuses, covered with Tommy, and very happy that I could get back into my own car alone after our brief conversation to compose myself and recover my stability.

I do not know if Bill had any near misses with me. For him to have pulled off a ten-year affair is testimony to . . . something. Both of us were willing and skilled adulterers. It sharpens the baser skills. And although the likelihood that you will get caught increases over time, you do get better at it. Getting better at it means you don't get caught. As Paul Theroux wrote in one of his travelogues, "It is very easy to plant a bomb in a peaceful, trusting place." That is what we both did. Then went and detonated it.

It is strange to me now that Bill and I should have turned out to be so very similar. We were polar opposites when we met in college. Socioeconomically, religiously, politically. Eventually we would argue politics over the dinner table. Our kids, once we had them, got a clearer view of both sides of every issue from Somalia to weapons of mass destruction to derivatives than ten newspapers could give them.

But that came much later. In the early days of our marriage, we were an embodiment of the notion that opposites attract. Still, I never quite understood what that was supposed to mean. There are so many kinds of opposites—which ones define you as a couple? Political opposites. Spiritual opposites. Clothes-folding opposites. Child-screaming-at opposites. Affection opposites. Restaurant-preference opposites. Intelligence-quotient and television-watching opposites. After really thinking this over, I came to the conclusion that an opposite is merely something that over time works itself around to being the same thing. My husband and I started out different but worked our way around to the same level of cunning, the same flare for adultery. And when it came to my third affair, with Terry, that flare came so easily that it was almost an instinct.

Terry and I were similar people from the beginning—affectionate, argumentative, passionate, in love with the outdoors. He had a core flair for action, usually expressed through hunting and fishing and the competition among men for trophies of all kinds.

We went from that afternoon walk along the canal path with my dog in the spring of 1991 to an almost constant togetherness that summer. We practiced archery nearly every day after work. (Bill would not get home from New York City until late. I worked in Princeton, much closer to our home.) We went out into the woods in the late afternoons to track Terry's tree stands or set new ones or just observe the transit of deer through the forests. We did not make love for the first few months. Terry was more conservative in that regard. I think he was trying to mitigate against his attraction by hanging out in otherwise innocent diversion. Though when it finally happened, I must say, he held nothing back.

We had been hunting all morning, having climbed by five A.M. into a tree stand in a forest bordering my parents' property. From that perch I watched the forest come alive. A wagon train of deer and their babies—some of them continually stepping out of line and bashing about like naughty kindergartners—paced under our stand and disappeared into the brush. We laughed, unable to keep quiet. It is astounding how noisy and active a forest is as the sun is coming up. I have never heard more screeching and chuckling and branch rubbing and warbling, squirrels and deer and birds and raccoons all orbiting the same thick stand of forest and taking raucous notice of one another. It was very primal. So when Terry and I got back to the barn on my parents' property we fooled around for the first time, persuaded, I think, by the feral exuberance of animals.

Our affair went indoors only occasionally. For me, one of our most poignant moments came after we had gone to hear the Philadelphia Orchestra perform Prokofiev's *Romeo and Juliet* suite that summer of 1991. Terry had never been to the symphony. It was a new kind of wild for him. It was a joy for me, too, watching a man who spent most of his life in camo gear respond to the gorgeous fusion of string instruments and concert hall acoustics and velvet seats. To the sense of occasion. Terry was as attentive in that seat as he had been the week before at full draw in his tree stand.

But as with the other affairs, the double life corroded every moment together. I longed to be in the woods with Terry. I didn't want to be at home with Bill. The opposing demands chafe at you, especially when one of them is verboten. One summer evening, I created a massive scene with Bill. I spun a fight out of nothing so that I could be out of the house at night. I was sick of fabricating excuses. You get tired of hearing your own lies. So after staging the fight, I stormed out the front door, yelling something about not returning for a week or a month, or ever. I called Terry to let him know I was available. But the stress of waiting for this availability was telling on him as well. He did not like the feeling of sidelining his own life just because I had a sudden night off. He was frustrated with the situation and said he would not come. I told him that I would, nevertheless, wait for him in town, a bottle of champagne on ice at the bar on the canal we occasionally went to.

Terry did not show up. Disgusted with myself and with the impossibility of our situation, I went outside and walked along Ferry Street to one of the wooden bridges that span the canal. I flung my unopened bottle of champagne over the side, the mood punctuated by the ka-*tunk* of it hitting the water. It sank into the murk. I'm sure it lies there still, buried in mud. I think of this every time I walk over the canal these days. It was good champagne, too.

As for the details and locations of Bill's various amours, I am not sure. I don't know about all of them, though I have found evidence enough of discrediting behavior over the years. There were always credit card receipts for "gentlemen's clubs" (is that name a deliberate irony?). Those receipts spiraled out of his pockets or showed up on his American Express statements. He had an affinity for strippers. Which of course works wonders on any young wife's esteem.

I do know when things began to go noticeably wrong with Bill. I saw a darker, alien side to him during his father's funeral, long before our children were born. It was an obvious departure from the man I met in college from that day forward. Bill's father was relatively young when he died, just fifty-three or fifty-four. At the funeral up in White Plains, we were standing at the back of the room and Bill was staring grimly into the middle distance. I looked over to him to see how he was doing. I put my hand on his arm. He leaned into me and hissed, almost threateningly, "Don't look at me." It was the smallest shutdown. Understandable given his grief, but crushing. I felt unnecessary to his life. Spouses are supposed to provide comfort. It was not wanted.

I think the divide really began widening from there. Considering what would follow in the years ahead, I believe that "Don't look at me" or its older brother, "Don't see me," became Bill's guiding credo. I was meant to observe it. Everyone was meant to observe it.

I wonder how useful it is, spelunking through our deep pasts looking for clues. Does any of this explain the origins of our behaviors or justify them? Mostly I think it just confuses the issue.

Looking at my life and at Bill's life in a general way, I suppose it does shine a dim lamp. The signs were all there. But it's sort of like a battlefield after the carnage, when the bodies are being pawed through by camp followers. Then it is easier to draw conclusions about how the battle went wrong, the artillery that missed its mark and hit something else instead, the horses that weren't supposed to be killed, too. All the grotesqueries of a failed pitched battle become obvious.

Likewise, it is easy to trace the arc of an adulterous relationship because it is so distinct from the mosh pit of daily life. You have your job and your marriage and your home and your responsibilities, and the affair has no place in any of it. It stands outside the realm, a true interloper, and its outlines are always blazing. But tracing the arc of a marriage's decline has none of that simplicity.

If I try to locate the mainspring of our demise, I look for the debris field. I can follow it all the way back through our wedding day and through our courtship and through our childhood, and I can tell myself I discern some pattern in the mess that I ought to have picked up on. In this way, after all, the *Titanic*'s final resting place was found. Oceanographers just followed the debris field back and back as it widened and grew fuller, until they found the broken hull.

But if you had stopped me in my hallway anytime during the eighteen years of our marriage and said, "How's your marriage going? Are you observing the signs? Have you taken note of the tilt of your sails and what's ahead of you?" I would probably have been mystified by the questions. I would have said, "Everything's going fine, it's been okay and it's still plugging along; why do you ask?" And gone forward on down the hallway, the significance lost on me.

If my family's drama and my devotion to reaction and my introduction to love with my high school boyfriend and every other euphoric moment and argument and melodrama along the way put me on this path, that's fine. But it made no difference to my awareness of it. I did not pick up on it when it might have mattered. Experience accrues. It molders in your head. It plays with your psyche in ways known and unknown, most of which will not become manifest until way past the time you need their lessons. This is how I've lived so far, utterly from the hip and without much forethought. Yet it has been dramatic. Fortune slay me, but that may have been just what I was looking for all along.

THE EFFICACY OF THERAPY

URING THE SPRING of 2005, in the months after finding out about Bill and Susan and their baby, I spent way too much time stumbling around the house absently while the boys were at school. I should have been knuckling down to deadlines and article interviews, but so many of my conversations devolved into sobfests. Not just the conversations with friends or family members. Even strangers. Even people in the grocery line. Even the formal reportorial conversations about police blotters and development plans and tax codes were precipitous. Let some Princeton Township official say "school budget" in the wrong tone and I went straight around the bend. I was a wandering, tearful mendicant holding my bowl out and asking for guidance.

Throughout my life books had always been a form of salvation for me, almost a religion. That spring, as I had since childhood, I would look to them for solace. Pull them down from the shelves. Feel the comfort of their heft. Smile at the little notations in the margins I had made from the easeful posture of my former life. But actual reading was beyond me, as it required a focus I did not have. There was no peace in me. I couldn't sit for two minutes in stillness. Even *Horton Hears a Who* would have posed a challenge.

One afternoon, I took down a book from my youngest son's shelf about outdoor skills. At age six he was too young to make any use of *The Special Air Service Survival Handbook,* which was published by a member of that elite unit of the British Army. But I bought him the book anyway for its thrilling chapter headings and its certainty that you could deal with a grizzly bear or a plane crash properly as long as you had the right information. There was a small disclaimer on the frontispiece warning readers that the survival techniques described were to be used "in dire circumstances" by individuals who were "at risk." So, yes, that would have been me at that point.

Hope flared. I wondered if Special Air Serviceman John "Lofty" Wiseman had a chapter for my predicament. The book was about survival, after all. He seemed to have included everything else. There were details on baiting spring spear traps and cooking shark meat. Offal had its moment in his book, and so did snow bollards. Wind direction and salt intake and the nesting habits of puff adders. There had to be some piece of survival advice I could stretch and recast and twist out of context to fit my situation so that I could embark on a course of survival and repair. I read for a full ten minutes, a geologic age to me then. There was nothing I could use, although I rose temporarily to the description of drowning. On land, Serviceman Wiseman wrote, one should use the Holger Nielsen method for reviving a victim who is prone on her stomach. I did spend a lot of time in that position, sobbing into the carpet.

I still find it odd that, apart from religious texts, there are no great, overarching practical guides to marital trauma. There are lots of aspirants but no definitive One. Since most of us are likely to face it more than once in our lives, it would seem like a good idea. A method of approach that says, Start here and proceed there. Not solace so much as a step-by-step workbook, a set of simple instructions on what to do with yourself. Even something along the lines of a Hasbro game board would suffice, with cards that you draw and game pieces that progress through a twisty series of questions and techniques. Pass Go. Get Out of Jail Free. Eat vegetarian chili. Breathe. Sometimes all you can do is fall back on a structure given you by someone else. A book detailing those options is at least as necessary as books about celestial navigation and amoebic dysentery. Emotional trauma is something we should be forced to take a formal course in during high school, sandwiched between advanced statistics and AP English. That would guarantee something useful out of all those years of schooling.

But there really isn't anything that serves. There is no primer on the exact kind of loss I felt. Which is too bad. I have a proactive personality, and the situation demanded that I do something. Go somewhere. Get guidance emanating from a source other than my damaged psyche or my friends and family, who were as likely to show up at Bill's office with torches and pitchforks as they were to come up with some salient bit of counsel. In the absence of a playbook, the default position of nearly everyone facing the betrayal of a spouse is the therapist's office. Therapists are the first responders.

Bill and I were no exception. We had been there before. In our household, the name of our therapist, Lillia, had practically become a verb. And the drive to her little fieldstone office was about as Pavlovian as you could get. I would point my car in her direction and the associations would immediately begin to flow.

I first met Lillia when I had been married for two years. I was twenty-nine and had begun the second of my affairs. The one after Tommy. The one with Steven in South Carolina. I knew this had to stop. I just didn't know how to cut off the fulmination of desire for others, yeasty and self-generating. I wondered if perhaps I was lacking something that was making me unhappy apart from the amorphous disappointments of my relationship with Bill. I wondered if there wasn't something deeper that was creating its own toxic influence on my behavior. I was in Lillia's office for two minutes, stomping righteously through a series of garden-variety childhood torments, when she asked, "Are you having an affair?"

This is what astonishes me about therapists. They draw those instantaneous conclusions about things the rest of us try mightily to hide. Or maybe that's just one of the main things that catapult us into therapy and they are used to it. I walked into Lillia's office hoping to hear how wonderful I was as a spouse, how aloof Bill was, how justified my conduct. I was a consumer of advice, and that was what I had paid to hear. "Yes," I squeaked. "Is it that obvious?" Apparently it was. The amount of dust I kicked up was clearly meant to obscure something.

Lillia told me that she would spend as many sessions as I wanted talking with me, helping me, plying me with questions enough to hang myself while I came to some sort of conclusion. But as for Bill, he would not be permitted in her office until I had confessed to the affair. That, she told me, would be unethical. It would be another form of betrayal. I was crushed with shame. I would imagine most therapists would find it . . . awkward . . . to conduct a session of therapy in which the most compelling factor was hidden from one of the spouses. Coming clean is essential to getting clean. To Lillia's everlasting credit, professional and personal, that is where the efficacy of therapy began and not one second before.

Still, it is efficacy of a limited nature. Inconvenient as it may be, therapists are actual human beings. They bring their own flaws and priorities to the session as they interpret your presenting relationship, so that it sometimes becomes one big amalgam of everyone's dysfunction. Sort of like hiring a knight in shining armor to help you claw your way out of a labyrinth, only to discover that his horse is lamer than yours. If your therapist was a child of divorce, if his own spouse cheated on him, if he cheated, if he is single, if he lives a hermetic life in the forest, eating herbs—you may not come to know any of this, but it will influence the direction of your therapy and the perspective that is brought to the table. Objectivity is the best goal, but I think it is not entirely obtainable.

At least there's a kind of safety in numbers. Bring a couple of minds to bear on your own tense situation and you just might hit on a course of action based on critical mass alone.

After the revelation of my second affair, Bill finally agreed to come to Lillia's office. I had already met with her several times alone in the lead-up to the confession and found all that very helpful. But helpful for me, personally. Not so much for the marriage. I don't think I would do that again if I intended to ask a spouse to join me, and I wouldn't recommend it.

I am sure many will disagree with me about this. But meeting with a therapist alone first sets up an expectation that will be disappointed if the therapist is any good. Namely, that the therapist will choose sides. Your side. That becomes part of the push-me, pull-you rapport. The prodigal spouse, the one who comes in after the foundation stone has been laid, is at a disadvantage. I don't see how it can be any other way, although if it's glaringly obvious, you should probably pick another therapist.

What I had tried to do before Bill came to Lillia's all those years ago was lay down my own story first. Not so that Bill would be adjudged wrong, but so that I would get off without a felony charge. The therapist is the judge and jury. I don't think anyone intends for it to be this way, but it is still a developing line. Couples compete for the therapist's summary judgment by trying to build the better case. I would try to prove that I was not nearly as awful as I might seem. Bill would try to prove that I was, in fact, much worse and no excuse on earth could diminish my guilt.

No doubt therapists are aware of this dynamic. They cannot help but be aware. We've seen it again and again in our lives, the dynamic of threes. It's the same brinkmanship that applies when your best friend in seventh grade brings along a second best friend to the vacation you've been invited on. The competition cranks up. The gloves are off. Someone will get left out of the threesome at least some of the time.

I have a close friend who started going to see a therapist with his wife after she told him she wanted a divorce. She had been to see the therapist alone several times, so of course the foundation stone dynamic had already kicked in. My friend perceived from the first minute of the first session that his wife had already set herself up as the victim. He cast about for his own footing, trying to tell his story. For that is what we do—we tell our stories. We plead them. We want our version codified by the authority of a person with a certificate. This is what he sought to do until the therapist asked him something that gave him serious pause: "Why do you want to stay with someone who doesn't want to be married to you?" Simple. Brutal. End of marriage. End of counseling session.

I may be wrong about this, but it is not my impression that this kind of blunt summation happens all that often. But it should. It should happen every time. Whether you want to remain together should be one of the first questions asked, and each spouse should try very hard to answer it. If the answer is, No, we do not want to work it out, or if one of the answers is, No, I do not want to work it out, then the therapist will have to find another couple on which to pin his or her billable hours.

I am not so cynical as to suppose that therapists want to make money off of beleaguered marriages. Forensic accountants, yes. Divorce lawyers, most decidedly yes. Therapists, no. Therapists genuinely want to help you, to help the couple, or at least to settle the ball long enough to figure out whether the union is even worth saving. This is why they go into the field in the first place. To behold, to grapple with, and to stand in awe over the messiness of couples. They actually like that stuff. They are the same kind of people who do well in MASH units or detox wards. They see mess as nobility.

Still, the therapy must be justified on a regular basis. And if you bluntly toss people out of your office because you realize the marriage is irredeemable, then you will have trouble paying the rent. You won't get to ply your trade. You won't get recompense for the great many hours you spent earning an advanced degree and poring through diagnostic books that will be useless when a couple like Bill and me walk through the door, years of adultery spread out under us like a stained blanket and years of adultery ahead. So many holes punched in the marriage.

I do not remember this question being asked during my first counseling session with Bill. I suppose we all dodged the issue out of sheer hopefulness. It was early in Lillia's career. It was early in our marriage. Yes, we could fix this. Yes, we wanted the challenge. Yes, she would show us how to proceed. So I walked down that Yellow

Brick Road lined with banal and pathetic excuses that forms the first line of defense for any cheater.

Bill came into Lillia's office the first morning mere days after hearing about Steven. He sat on the couch with his hands interlocked behind his neck, a posture of affected calm that actually made him look more tortured than he meant to look. He did not want to be there. He didn't see the point of discussing all of this with a third party. And since he knew I had already met with Lillia on several occasions, he viewed her as complicit. As if the two of us had plotted some strategy to get me out of trouble and were simply seeing it through.

Lillia gingerly made a first attempt to reach through Bill's resistance. She asked me to talk about why I had cheated. Barely had one sentence come out of my mouth—something along the lines of I didn't feel loved—when Bill's hands snapped out of their locked position. He sat forward, bolted forward almost. And said in a rage, "I am *not* going to listen to this."

And he meant it. Because over the next thirty minutes or so before the session ended with Bill walking furiously out of Lillia's office and out through her sitting room and out through the door with the little bell on it to the parking lot, where he went directly to our car and climbed in and slammed the door, I said a lot of apparently stupid things. Stupid because they were among the last things Bill needed to hear, among the last things any spouse needs to hear when he has just found out he has been betrayed.

I heard myself saying, for instance, that I cheated because my lover understood me better. The spark was gone out of my marriage. The sex was no longer thrilling. I was bored. My needs weren't being met. One or another version of these excuses crossed my lips like so many dark, knee-jerk Hallmark card sentiments. I'm not saying these weren't legitimate, because on some level they were. Just that they didn't legitimize what I was doing. Had I believed they were a solid rationale, my stomach wouldn't have dropped on the way out the door to Tommy's apartment each time I visited him. I wouldn't have felt the need to shower after a liaison and before climbing back into the marital bed. I wouldn't have felt as if a train had struck me in the small of the back whenever Bill asked casually, So, Wen, what did you do today?

I wouldn't have hid it all. I wouldn't have needed to.

During that first session with Lillia and Bill, I should have seen the warning signs in Bill's agitated posture. Instead I strove urgently to justify myself. I saw a flash of hope on the horizon and I galloped blindly toward it, kicking up clods of rationalization. Someone else was buying into my excuses. My therapist, God love her, followed what I was saying with a beseeching kindness in her eyes. She understood. She wanted me to go on. So I did. I began many sentences with the phrase "I never meant to . . ." But one look at the hollow-eyed, defeated form of my spouse sitting next to me would have reminded me that such claims simply amplified his pain.

I think most therapists use these excuses as a place to start, a way to pick up clues and climb in deeper, get to know the couple sitting on the couch. Many therapists move through them with a kind of mathematical rigor. Because the therapist does, in fact, understand them. They make sense in a superficial way, and they've been tossed around so much that they are almost a received wisdom. Spouses do feel unloved, do feel bored, do think the lover understands them better or is at least more willing to act that way for the sake of getting laid.

What I think I should have been told—what I think any adulterer should be told—is this: If your needs weren't being met, you ought to have communicated them. If the spark was gone and this bugs you, find it again or get out. Is sex ever really boring, really? And you know where the passion went—it went into your lover's bed, that is where you took it. And your lover really understood you better only because you were answering the front door in a thong.

This, I think, would level the playing field in the first fraught inning, when it counted most. It is the truth, after all. It would be a way of outing the betrayer, of calling his or her bluff. There are few safer places to lay it on the line than in a therapist's office. Presumably that is what you are there for.

How deep the irony, then, when these same excuses were immediately hauled forth by Bill about three years later when he sat in the opposite seat. It was right after I had found out about his first affair, the one with the stripper. Lacking that Hasbro game board to fit the situation, I could think of only one course of action: Get us both back to Lillia and figure out how to handle this reverse affair. Back Bill and I tramped to her office wearing opposite suits of armor. I was aggrieved. Bill was guilty. And he offered up the same pack of excuses I had tried to use, almost to the word. He didn't feel loved. There was no spark in our marriage. Anne understood him better.

I could have thrown up. I could not hear it. I was a storm of wrath because Bill used the very excuses he had once repudiated. And like Bill many years before, I was being asked by Lillia to consider their worth. I felt defeated in every way—as cheater and as cheated.

It proves how facile and flexible these excuses are. They arise out of nowhere and find us wherever we are, like field mosquitoes.

When they do, we deploy them quickly and reflexively, without really thinking about what they mean. Now that I have been on both ends of infidelity, I want to throw out a challenge to find some other way of approaching the early phases of finding out. Perhaps the "spark has gone out" drift works at some later point, once things have calmed down and you are willing to roll up your sleeves. But in the raw, beginning phases of trying to find your way back to someone you have wronged, little suffices except I'm sorry, I'm sorry, I'm sorry, I'm sorry, I'm sorry.

To me, one of the strengths of therapy is also one of its biggest drawbacks. Therapy wants to get to the bottom of things. It wants to figure out your life. It wants to plunge back into your childhood and drag it forward to apply like a balm to the irksome patterns you've developed since then. All this is very good for the individual, but it doesn't do a lot for a couple in real crisis.

I don't see what difference it makes if your parents treated you as if you were an idiot child or as if you were the Sun King. It has a huge bearing on who you've become. But a flailing couple doesn't need the full-court press of deep therapy. Not right away. They need to know how they should handle right now. How should they deal with each other on the way home in the car, in the kitchen eating dinner, on the phone tomorrow when he's at work, in front of the children, alone in bed. Point to a marital map. Show us where we are. Show us where we'll go if we get this right.

Every time I hear someone—on television, on the radio, in a book, at a restaurant table next to me—talking about love or marriage or relationships, I thrill to the hope of some real, honest information. I lean in as if I'm going to hear a secret. I incline forward to eavesdrop on whatever they are going to say. I always want answers—

for all of it. What turns us on. What drives us. What drove us. What drove over us. I think the reason so much advice disappoints is that it tries to be too optimistic about all of our chances. And too much optimism puddles around the truth, drowning it.

I think for most married people, and certainly for me, the truth is a little more difficult and a little less appealing. You wander around in the marital labyrinth and mark out the best path you can in enclosure, without the long view. In the end it may look like a very stupid path indeed, something like a lost cow would trace wandering through a bog. But to me, the hopelessness of that path makes me love it all the more. And the honesty of that hopelessness makes me want to try harder, to put my shoulder into it. To piss off the gods who threw marriage at us as a joke and prove them wrong.

It was in early 2005, around a month after finding out about the continued presence of Susan in Bill's life and the reality of their son, that I had a session with another therapist who used a direct route. She practiced therapy as the crow flies. I had called a random number in the yellow pages for a therapist and found one on Stony Brook Road, near our home. Lillia was a soothing counselor. But she went back and forth through my life, through Bill's life. And we were in crisis. We needed straightforward, no-nonsense advice. Or maybe we just needed a whole raft of help.

So I made an appointment that night for Bill and me with the Stony Brook Road therapist. I told her a few specifics over the phone so she would have a chance to think about her approach. I told her we didn't need the dynamic of compassionate understanding that we'd seen before. Don't take sides or ask us to justify our behaviors or burrow into our histories. Just help us, I said. Tell us where to go.

Unfortunately, I showed up at her office alone. After agreeing during the day that he would go with me, Bill later refused. He said he needed to be at work late, but he was just dodging, because when I phoned his office later, he was not there. He did not meet me that night. He did not come home. He was one of the disappeared, again. My parents arrived at my home to babysit for the duration of the session. They said, Go anyway. Go alone. See what she has to say to you. So I went alone. I showed up at that therapist's office as insubstantial as a cirrus cloud, weak with grief. She took one look at me and said, This is what you need to do.

One thing was obvious to all of us from the beginning of finding out: Bill needed to have a relationship with his new son. It killed me to admit this, but I knew it was a necessity. If we were going to stay together, as I hoped we would, it simply had to be. I am a mother. I knew that parents need their children as much as children need their parents. Bill's new baby was not yet a year old. He needed him. Our sons were six and nine. They needed him. We were married. I needed him. I couldn't have cared less whether Susan needed him. It did not occur to me that he needed her. All I saw was that my family depended on our ability to work this out.

The therapist answered with admirable restraint. The first thing we had to do, she said, was work out the logistics. Pretend we were planning visitation rights. When Bill would see his third child and under what circumstances. What level of intrusion Susan was allowed in our lives. If she could call our home whenever she wanted to talk with Bill in the service of their child. What we would do on holidays. How much money Susan would receive for support. What involvement my sons would have. Figure it out, write it down, hand out copies to everyone. Like a partnership, albeit the kind cemented during a hostile takeover.

I thought this was great advice. But if I say that settling each of these questions was like flaying myself with a dull blade, I offer some idea of the exquisite torture. I was a howling dog of despair and wayward intention. I veered endlessly between trying to be fair about Susan and Bill's shared parenthood and hating Susan and Bill. I bought Bill's new baby a baby blanket one day. And the next, when Bill showed me a first photo, I said, "My sons are cuter." (It was simply the first thing that came to mind and, under the circumstances, I think the most restrained opinion I could offer.) I called Susan on the phone with Bill beside me in the car and said we could work together. And then I swore the most damning curses at her under my breath. I vowed to be decent toward everyone involved. And then I would take the deal down in a torrent of tears and fury. I wanted to work it out, but I hated having to work it out. I bemoaned our family's fate. It took most of that year, from the finding out at the end of January until early December 2005, for me to even adequately process our new reality, to say nothing of how my sons would handle it.

We had decided not to discuss this with them until the situation had stabilized a bit. So for several months they remained unaware of their father's extracurricular family. I can only say that during that time, my sons would come often upon their mother in tears—in the laundry room, in the garage, over my computer. Anywhere that I found myself alone for more than two seconds. I'm sure they were bewildered. I would just use the "Mommy is tired, sweetheart" excuse. They were little boys. I doubt it sufficed. But I did not think they would even be able to grasp what was going on.

Based on the therapist's prescription, we had agreed that Bill would see his new baby every Saturday and Sunday morning for ninety minutes each and once during the week on Wednesday evening. It was a lame schedule, yes, but it was a start. It allowed us to take the first lurching laps through the test pattern. But I did not do this at all well. I would watch those ninety minutes tick away and was incapable of much else for the duration. I would start calling Bill's cell phone at ninety-one minutes. I would stare at the top of the driveway, waiting for his car to appear. I would torture myself with all the possibilities of what he and Susan were doing at that house one mile away.

I never went back to that other therapist. I did not want to go alone. Instead I went back to Lillia. Bill wanted no part of therapy. We had only about four sessions together through our whole marriage. But I needed the counseling. I saw Lillia as often as I could afford. I scribbled her encouragements on the backs of business cards and stuffed them in my pockets, in my wallet, in my checkbook. They would fall out at the most inopportune times, but I would catch sight of the little messages fluttering to the ground and I would take heart.

I don't remember most of what she said, then or when I first went to see her with Bill when we were twenty-nine. I do remember lots of questions, though: How did our spouse's unhappiness make us feel, what improvements did we think we could make, what would have been a better option, was your mother loving, what was your order in the family of siblings? Questions so earnest that they always seemed to be leading us somewhere. But they never did. My experience of therapy was like wandering in a great fogbound circle. If you walked fast, it just got bigger and the curve receded. If you plodded, it shrank and became claustrophobic. But it always retained the same shape and wound you up at the same spot, pregnant with knowledge of yourself but no clue about how to fix the marriage.

One option I rejected was the use of meds. I still find it mildly disturbing that so many therapists prescribe them. Prozac, Lexapro, Zoloft, Paxil. There is even one called Sarafem, which sounds like an Italian liqueur or a honeymoon resort. Not by accident. These names were dangled in front of me by many people that year. They would look at my wasted frame and say, You should go on something.

Early in my reporting career, I wrote a series of articles on mental illness. Among the places I visited was the Trenton Psychiatric Hospital, which is on a green, tree-lined road outside the city across from the region's other exclusive entity, the Trenton Country Club. I spent a whole day at that hospital, where patients were tied down in chairs, whacking at their own heads, tearing at their clothes. I had conversations with patients who were completely rational until suddenly they were not. It was a haunted building.

The story also led me to a family whose oldest son, David, had been diagnosed with schizophrenia at the age of nineteen. He lived in a group home with three other men on the edge of Ewing, New Jersey. I formed an attachment with them. Long after the story was published, I used to go over to their house once a month to cook them big vats of spaghetti and sit on their couch, listening to them talk. David drank black coffee out of a plastic Slurpee cup and kept a Polaroid camera on his bedside table. He said he used it to take photographs of his room at night so he would see that the voices he heard calling out to him were not really there.

At no point in my sadness did I resemble these lost and shattered souls. I was situationally depressed, which is not the same thing.

David, his housemates, those patients at the psychiatric hospital—these were the people who needed the full support and research and assistance that the pharmaceutical industry could give them. They needed the meds. I do not think meds were manufactured for cuckolds. But there isn't much of a market in schizophrenia, so the peddlers of drugs for an affluent nation looked elsewhere for their customers. Hello, suburbia.

Of course, meds help a lot of people, and that's commendable. But I was very clear about wanting to get through the situation on my own steam, or at least to go over the falls on my own steam. I wanted to know that I could do it without medication. It had to do with obtaining the skills, finally, to deal with a major crisis. I had a happy childhood. It did nothing for the nest of snakes I was confronted with midway through my life. I figured it was high time to learn to deal. So I looked at my unhappiness the way I looked at fever, a symptom of something wrong. The unhappiness, like the fever, is present because it has a job to do. It flags your attention. It calls your focus home. You struggle through it, and with its help you recover, eventually.

As it turns out, therapy came in all forms. It came from my friends. It came from my parents, who rushed over from their home more times than I can count. It came from my sister, who flew to my side on the night of discovery, and my brother, who was the first to call Bill that day in January 2005 to tell him, Don't do anything rash, because your family needs you.

It came from a neighbor I ran across at CVS who grabbed hold of my sleeve out of concern and would not let go until I had explained my wild appearance, my pale visage, my sudden weight loss. It came from a yogic friend who told me that I could surmount this challenge but that I needed to manifest a "World Series" of peace and mindfulness. (I hate baseball.) It came from the owner of a tree service who visited one afternoon to give me a work estimate and walked my dog instead. It came from a high school friend, Zane, who had already trekked through a divorce of his own, and another, Robert, who was just starting.

If I were to write a therapy instruction card for myself right now, like a set of directions for CPR or snakebites that is printed on heavy stock and handed out in park offices, it would have these survival notes on it for the early stages of betrayal's grief. I would offer these few tactics to myself:

One, everything doesn't have to be solved in one session. Particularly while the air is choked with smoke and rancor. Learn to be still in the therapist's office so that you can absorb what you need to absorb.

Two, on the other hand, try to be clear about what you need. You are paying for this advice, so get it. In crisis, you don't need to troll through your childhood. You need a handful of simple, clear instructions for how to get yourself and your spouse through the early stages. Therapists are the experts, so call on them to use it judiciously.

Three, remember that it is the two of you who matter most. It is you and your spouse against the world, not you and your therapist. An early awareness of this ought to help clear the path ahead.

Four, on the other hand, you have to step up to the plate. You have to take some responsibility for the efficacy of your therapy. Put some serious energy into it. I admit to being lethargic or overly daft in the therapist's office. Fix it! Fix it! That is what I wanted, which seems silly to me now. It was the wrong thing to expect, I think.

Five, be willing to hear that you've screwed up royally and need to make amends. And then make amends. Use with caution the tactic of calling in reinforcements in the form of excuses. If you want to save the marriage, nothing works better than a pure expression of remorse.

Six, there are many ways to get out of the woods. If you're chasing the wrong path or cycling endlessly through the same patch of ground, find another way out, find another therapist. Find someone who is going to give you the help you need, as distinct from the help you want. Sob into the laps of friends and family. The paid therapist is for concrete counsel.

Seven, and most important, understand that you can bear it. You will not want to. But flailing about looking for relief is only going to make it worse, in the very way that screaming or panicking during labor and delivery will only sap your energy. Sit with it for a moment. Let it knock you down like a rogue wave and then watch it roll on. I now know that this can be done. You can stay still through it.

Therapy had its value, but it remained a stubbornly limited one. Even in concert with all of our best intentions, therapy could not rescue our marriage. I'm not sure that therapy can rescue any marriage. The profession generally implies otherwise, and this strikes me as an exaggerated claim. It seems better to know that going in.

After all the smoke of 2005 cleared, I found a better way to look at therapy. I look at it now as an almost literal course of solace, like a class you might take in school on how to heal. A place to open the floodgates and have the tide of grief managed by a paid expert who will not be worn out—as friends and family can be—by the emotional demands of the crisis. A therapist will listen and listen and

listen, which is one of the things you need most. Rescuing the marriage seems a tall order. But there is a chance that therapy can rescue you. Perhaps the expectation should end there. It does seem
like enough.

THE OTHER WOMAN, THE OTHER MAN

HOME WRECKER. HARPY. Cheater. Bitch. Player. Betrayer. Betrayed. I have used all of these words and been them, too. I have visited both poles of infidelity and found the terra not so very incognita at either end. I have been the Other Woman and I have been at the Other Woman's mercy. I have known many of the Others that go with adultery—the other man, the other friend, the other brother, the other mom, even the other other man, the one as aggrieved as me. Then and now, all these other people animated a jumble of intimate, combat-locked motives. For me, this was never more so than when it came to Susan.

It is an odd relationship that I have with Susan these days. I wonder if she knows how well I understand her. Not just what drove her to an affair with my husband, but the whole gestalt of her. How she fell into the affair unknowingly because my husband did not tell her he was married; how she found out too late that he was not a single man; how once she found out, she no longer cared because she was in love with him. My own experience as the other woman has given rise to a viewpoint from which I can say, now, I know well how it happens.

I got an e-mail from Susan in 2005 only a few weeks after finding out about the two of them. Once I read through it, I thought she had taken a crashing leave of her senses. And, I admit it, I wanted to get in the ring and mix it up, an old-fashioned sort of retribution in which I would get to bash until sorry the person jointly responsible for taking my family down. Of course, this did not happen. We no longer live in an age of frontier justice. I guess that's a good thing for the general maintenance of order in the streets, but for me I'm not entirely convinced. Some days I still want a pugilist's satisfaction. I sometimes want bruised knuckles.

Time and time again I was warned off going near Susan. "Have nothing at all to do with her," my friend Elsa told me. "She won't listen to you and you'll just get in trouble." Alas, I was unable to stay away entirely. There was a centripetal pull to Susan that I found irresistible. She had all the answers to my sad questions: how they met, how many business trips she had been on with Bill, who bought her the home she is living in now. And most generally, What was her sway over my husband? And once I got her e-mail, I had an answer.

It was a strangely cheerful note, something along the lines of what you might receive from Mrs. Claus if she ever undertook a letter campaign of her own. It was resolutely optimistic. It had a Dorothy of Oz quality to it, as if Susan were writing it with the same casual oblivion Dorothy displayed when dropping houses on people and killing them off. There was no remorse in her e-mail. My cooperation was invited in the most assuming way. The whole situation was laid out with brutal logic, but cloyingly. I got a cavity just reading it.

I did not realize then what I was dealing with. But I ought to have. As a onetime Other Woman during my affair with Steven, I remember well the feeling of drunken power, the range of lethal weapons at my command, my belief in my equality with the wife. I do not think Susan acted with quite this level of impunity, although she was ruthless in her own way. But in my own case, I was only too aware of it. My affair with Steven, who was married with daughters, gave me an unexpurgated view of myself as the other woman. It was not a pretty sight.

I never met Steven's wife or saw her in person. During one of our weekends together, I noticed a photograph of her in his car tucked up behind the driver's-side visor. Before I pulled it down, I asked his permission to look at it. Even while I was abusing her status, I felt there was a certain fraught etiquette owing to her. The Other, whether it's a man or a woman, is always in a weird position, triumphant and imperiled at the same time. On that edge there is no room for a misstep. There must be some level of respect paid to the spouse. He or she was, after all, there before and is there still. The prior claim deserves acknowledgment. And I had known from the very first afternoon of meeting him that Steven was married. He told me straight out later that night, and I told him the same thing. It was as if we were settling that score before moving on to the more important business of sleeping together.

In the photo, Steven's wife was standing in the surf in South Carolina, wearing cutoff jeans that revealed just how gorgeous and fit she was. When I first saw that photo, I thought, as everyone does, What is there to improve on? Why seek anyone else?

"Because I want to be with you," Steven told me when I asked. That is the power of the Other. It doesn't matter how beautiful the spouse is, how rich, how funny or smart, how dug in your lover is at home, how surrounded by children and pets and mortgage payments that underscore their legal bond. Steven wanted me, and it nullified, at least temporarily, everything else that he had with her.

Once this was made clear to me, I reveled in it. I did not feel better than his wife, but I felt different. I was not her. That is all the advantage you need during an affair. I was not encumbered with children. I could run with Steven at will. I lavished him with affection. I stayed out with him all night. We went boating. We drank, we ate. We were never too tired for sex. In short, there were no limits except the ones imposed by his marital obligations—and apparently, during that one week, they were not all that limiting. Mine was an annihilating advantage, unfair in every way. I was aware of that even then.

What I mostly thought about Steven's wife in my young ignorance was that she was foolish. Here was this beautiful man, full of life and vitality, curious for the whole world and everything in it. I couldn't comprehend why she left him alone so often. It made no sense that she wasn't constantly out with him in a constant state of bliss more or less constantly. Bill and I did not yet have children, so there was a great deal more I couldn't comprehend—like how much children anchor you to a home. And make it less likely that you can stay out all night. And go boating whenever you feel like it. And have anything that resembles a self-driven life. Part of me thought she was to blame. If she's not paying attention, then I am her own fault. If she's not loving him, well, then I will. This is the prevailing mood of the Other.

Sometimes I even imagined Steven's wife would not have cared had she known. This too was part of the bacchanalia of self-justification. Many women I know joke about how other women are welcome to their husbands. I do not know if men do this, but women do. They joke about how a mistress would relieve them of the obligation of having sex they don't crave all that much anymore. It makes me wince. I do not think they really know what they are saying. But

I bought into it then. I thought, I am doing Steven's wife a favor. She can now stay at home with the kids and read *Goodnight Moon* and do the gardening. I'll occupy her husband, take him off her hands, and send him home too exhausted to paw at her. Oh yes, it's a sick logic that serves the Other.

But if truth be told, I did not spend much time thinking about Steven's wife at all. Her feelings, her love for her husband, the lives of their girls, the state she would be in should she discover my presence in their world, hardly entered the tight orbit of my consideration. A surfeit of empathy would have gotten in the way. And if I wasn't going to extend it to my own spouse, I certainly wasn't going to extend it to someone else's. She was on my mind when Steven was preparing to come north to visit me. I wondered what excuse he would use and whether she would become suspicious. That's when I thought of her. Because she had the possibility of thwarting our plans. That is the only time she entered my mind forcefully.

Steven and I did not discuss his wife, or only to the extent that I would ask where she was that day or that evening such that he could be out and wandering around with me. We did not trash her. We didn't sit around and talk about how lousy our marriages were. The phrase "I wish she were more like you" never crossed Steven's lips, or anything like it. He didn't wish for that. He wanted her to be her and me to be me. And I felt the same for him.

I was crazy about Steven, but I never considered leaving my marriage for him, and there was not the slightest evidence that he wanted that himself. Our separate marriages were our separate homes, literal and figurative. They removed the necessity of laying down claims on each other, and that was relieving. Both of us already had claims. The affair could be something else. It was a vacation, a temporary, exotic port of call. The mutual understanding of this incontrovertible fact was what made Steven such a good Other Man.

Besides, I had no desire to make the journey from Other Woman to Woman, meaning the woman he marries after he splits with his wife. If there is a more teetering cliff edge on which to establish your happiness, I do not know it. To go from the desired, semi-attainable Other to the woman he comes home to each night after leaving behind, ignominiously, everyone and everything he originally loved, including quite possibly small children—I would rather clean bilge tanks in a container ship on rough seas. It seems you have more chance of fulfilling that role.

In my view, crushing, worrisome regret lies in wait for the single woman or the single man who has an affair with a married spouse, pulls the spouse away, and then marries him or her. As the new spouse, you would have to help justify the sacrifice of the first marriage on a too-often basis. And if you or he or both don't cheat again, you will end your days worrying that it's about to happen. When you are betraying a spouse, one of the things you demonstrate most emphatically is how untrustworthy you are. Not much of a basis on which to hang a new marriage.

It was the same with Tommy and with Terry, although they were both single. There were no expectations of a future with me for either of them. I remember Tommy saying in one of his rare moments of gravity that he did not want me leaving my husband for him. His warning carried this subtle but unmistakable subtext: I am here to sleep with you and have fun with you, and apart from that you can count on nothing. What's more, the potential wreckage of your union is your own responsibility.

Neither Tommy nor Steven nor Terry had been with a married woman before me, so far as I knew. So that wasn't necessarily part of their mission. But it may have been part of the allure. A married woman is committed elsewhere. From the Other Man perspective, I was unlikely to make demands about the years ahead. I was uninterested in buying drapery and pillows together. I didn't want to have their children. I wanted something altogether different that the Other Man was only too happy to supply. Not just sex and lots of it. But romance. And fun. Fun like when you were younger. Fun like when you were single and had no care apart from finding the coolest, most exciting thing to do next. Marriage blows that out of the water. The Other brings it back.

But Tommy, for one, had significant drawbacks as an Other Man. He was single. He answered to no one. I never knew where he was half the time, and he did not offer any explanations. I was married. I could make no justifiable demands on him. If I could not find him, then he could not be found. There would be no explanation forthcoming. Or there would be a shrug, which said: I am single, you are married, and if you want to know where I was, you might as well go home to your husband.

The need for him to account for anything—his whereabouts, his plans, his feelings for me—was simply nonexistent. This is hard on a romance even when there is no legitimacy to it. I was the guilty party, and that dissolved all the normal relationship rules. An Other Man who is also married is devoted to you for the duration of the affair. An Other Man who is single has the whole world at his bidding, and you as well, awash in jealousy. You can like it or you can leave. But you cannot reasonably lay down any claims of monogamy when you are returning home shortly to climb into bed with your spouse.

Somewhere below the surface of the Other's amiable personality also lurks sanctimony. If the Other is not married, then a smaller share of guilt attaches to him. The Other can carry that guilt more easily because he is betraying a stranger rather than the person to whom he gave a lifelong vow. I remember an afternoon during my affair with Terry when this became clear. We were down at the shore for the night, sleeping at my parents' shore home without their knowledge. As we were climbing into bed, I said something about how they would be destroyed had they known what I was doing, and in their space, too. Terry said, "Well, yeah. You probably shouldn't be doing this."

As the married person, you are wrong coming and going, even from the viewpoint of the person sleeping with you. The censure may be well deserved, but it is still a lonely place to be.

When you are on the Other side—as the Other Woman or Other Man—it is a place of high disdain. Or so I found. During the span of months that I was with Steven, there were whole forests being leveled in South Carolina by one of the South's largest and most aggressive paper companies. Steven and I used to hike through those forests. The blast corridors were Dantesque, with a wreckage of trees in all directions. I think that is an apt metaphor for the Other. We saunter along, throwing down trees, sowing wreckage, and, Gatsby-like, leave the consequences for someone else to clean up.

I was an Other Woman before I knew what it really meant, before it had been visited on me. What surprises me in retrospect was my total lack of remorse. My complete detachment from and disinterest in the Other Spouse and her children, whom I was also betraying. I wonder what I would have done had I met Steven's wife face-to-face—then and now. I remember what I was like when I first found out about Susan during that phone call to Atlantic City. I was a spitting harpy. However justified I thought myself, that was who I became. If I had had to confront Steven's wife under those conditions, with her raving at me, I have no idea how I would have responded. Then.

Now. I would apologize. I would bow my head. I would end the affair. I would be abject with remorse. But ask me if that imagined remorse would have been enough to prevent my having an affair with her husband in the first place. That is where I lean over and switch off the screen without answering. And turn, instead, and for illustration, to Susan.

By February 2005, one month after finding out about her, I had spoken to Susan just once while Bill sat beside me in our car. I wanted to talk with her. I don't even know what kind of impulse that is, but I wanted to get the whole mess out on the floor so we could see what it looked like. On impulse, Bill agreed. He dialed her home number. Hearing the first few sentences of their easy exchange was awful—just the way she answered so casually, revealing years of answering the phone in this very manner, with him on the other end—but I had asked for this. Bill handed me the phone, and she and I talked about our imminent cooperation.

She sounded . . . nice. She thanked me for the baby blanket I had sent her son. I mumbled something about let's work this all out calmly. We kept it brief, Bill sitting uneasily beside me, clearly worried that she or I would say something that would implicate him in some new way. And there were plenty of ways, as he had not been honest with either of us. When I handed him back the phone, he simply said good-bye to her. I did not know what she understood their relationship to be at that point.

But I assumed—blindly—that he had called an end to it and was back home with the boys and me for good and that their relationship was confined to parenting their baby. I thought it was understood that she would back off and yield the floor, retire gracefully into the middle distance, and see him only as regarded their child. I thought she was taking the news remarkably well for someone who had been his girlfriend for ten years.

The next day, though, I got the e-mail. Among other things, it demonstrated that Susan was not going anywhere anytime soon.

The e-mail began with a reference to our conversation in the car the day before and suggested that this had already put us on a road of repair. She was looking forward to working out an amicable solution with me. In the history of understatements, there can be few to match this one.

It went on for a full page, and so did I, tearing through every word. She emphasized the children's needs and the presence of so many unconventional families in the world. As if perhaps the situation my sons now found themselves in might offer a broadening, life-enhancing experience if only they embraced it fully. I felt as if I was being asked to register my gratitude for her contributions to our lives.

As Susan wrote, she declaimed a kind of propaganda that would have made Chairman Mao sit up and beg. Particularly amusing was her insistence that we—meaning, no doubt, I—should accept the difficult situation Bill found himself in. How hard it was for him to have so many responsibilities and a new baby to boot. Poor Bill. So many families, so many challenges, so many alibis to work out. And then she told me that she promised to make sure Bill would feel at ease spending time with my sons.

Here, I have to pause to thank Susan for allowing my husband to spend time with us. I can only assume she would do the same for any additional families Bill happens to have. But anyway.

Susan added that she was sure I would want to give Bill the flexibility to spend time with his new child. She was also certain that I would be comfortable allowing Bill to spend an equal amount of time with all of his children without any guilt or pressure or aggravation from me.

Enough of this. That's all I can take of Susan's e-mail even now. The rest of it goes on in the same vein, an instant classic in the art of perverse logic. It is bad enough that I hang on to this missive out of a need to recall how it was all laid out for me. Worse still to parse through it, line by perky line.

But given my own background as an Other Woman, I should not have been that surprised at the tone Susan took. It was all there: the air of being on a par with me, the presumption of my goodwill, the complete lack of remorse, the inability to comprehend the hell she had handed me and my boys. I do not think we had been much considered when stacked against her own needs and the needs of her child.

What is a spouse to do with such a letter? Even reading it now, six years later, I want to burn it. Pour the acid of my hurt over it and hurl it. I saw red mostly because Susan had invoked my sons and put them alongside hers as if it were the most natural thing in the world. I was not prepared for this. Every maternal feeling revolted. I would never—I still don't—see her child as on a par with my sons. For me, their interests will always come before anything her child needs. My e-mail response to Susan later that afternoon reflected that. I believe there were various words beginning with the letter "f" and one or two of an equally damning nature. How could I have been any different?

Then again, how could she? The Other Woman or Man does not necessarily believe she or he is an interloper in the intimate space of a marriage. This is what makes them do what they do. Especially when they have been treated over the years to the solicitation of the lover, as Susan had. For a decade she enjoyed money, gifts, airline tickets, sex, love, and promises for the future. Our marital funds fueled a lot of the things they did—Disney World trips, house improvements, flights to Mississippi with him.

The Other considers him- or herself on a level with the spouse because that is where the Other has been put. They believe, most of them, that the neglect that has brought the three of you to this brink is largely your own fault. They even think they have done you a favor. I thought all of this toward Steven's wife. Susan felt all of this toward me. It was a tangle upon a tangle upon a tangle.

Right from the beginning I was desperate to see her. I wanted to know what she looked like. Where she had been in her life. What kind of a person she was. How she came to meet Bill, because to this day I do not know that salient detail. I had some of these questions answered eventually, but they were of a shifting nature. I still do not know whether any of the things I was told about her by Bill are true.

But on the afternoon that I finally did meet Susan in person, the difference between us was almost comical. We were nothing alike. I was wearing a surfer board skirt and Dr. Martens sandals, a ripped T-shirt, and a tan, my hair curly with pool chlorine and my face absent of makeup per usual. She was in an ironed button-down white shirt open to cleavage, thick makeup, a serious pile of coiffed hair, nails done (toenails, too), tight designer jeans, and high wedge sandals of the kind that were fashionable that summer. And she was small—about six inches shorter than me. And I thought, What is there to choose between us?

We had agreed to meet at a local park, over by the playground, so that the children could see one another and put faces to their new Alice in Wonderland reality. For me it was an attempt to begin to introduce the boys to the future drift of their lives and the presence of their father's new child out there beyond our home. I could think of no other way to do it than to have them meet. Up to then, the situation did not make much sense to my sons—Dad has a what? With who? I wanted them to begin to know.

Susan had brought gifts for my boys. I had brought a gift for her baby. The whole meeting was conducted with strained cheer, a surfeit of forced optimism. My older son pushed the child on a swing halfheartedly. My younger son milled around and stared obliquely, as in, I don't get this party at all.

Later, as the boys and I drove home, I said to them, That went pretty well, don't you think? Their responses were muted, almost bored. They wanted to go out for ice cream. Already their attentions had turned to what was more interesting to them and what made more sense: ice cream, home, Mom. I do not think they had any sense of a relation to that child. Which was fine with me. I would provide the opportunity, not the persuasion. As for me, driving home from that meeting, I felt as if someone had switched on a set of beaters in my stomach and blended my organs all to hell.

That was just the beginning. The question of choice drove me mad that summer. It took ten months to solve, but it felt like an ice age of time. I did not know if Bill was choosing between us, if he had already chosen, and what was happening between them. I was a fool throughout. He was impossible to pin down on the subject. But Susan was decent to me from the point of finding out. She never spilled the whole truth of their ongoing affair, but she didn't lie about it anymore, either. She walked a careful line between two centaurs. It must have taken a ration of courage to deal with Bill and me as we were in those early days of the discovery.

In the late summer of 2005, I called Susan on my own, desperate to know if she and Bill were still sleeping together. Obviously, I had asked Bill. He denied it and said he was back with me. But the evidence of their continuing affair was everywhere. Bill would disappear for days and be unreachable. He wouldn't call. He would claim his cell phone had run out of power. He lost his recharge cord. His phone at work was broken. Or he was out of town on business and forgot to leave me the name of the hotel and then couldn't communicate it because his cell phone, his charger, his car phone, the hotel phone, and all the phones within walking distance were inoperable, as also his computer and every satellite servicing his area.

Or he just didn't answer his phone and it rang and rang and rang. I was coming unglued.

On the afternoon that I called Susan, I wanted to know one thing: Were they still having sex? That would have been proof enough that their affair continued, obviously, and I needed proof. I needed something strong enough to knock me out of my loop of disconnect. Because in my stupidity I had honestly assumed the affair was over. I thought she was in the picture only because of the baby. That is what I had been told by my husband. Apparently, she had been told the same thing about me. I was coming to see that

Bill was telling everyone whatever version would secure him a quick exit and enable him to duck the whole zone of wreckage.

When I called her that day, Susan didn't answer plainly either, but she did at least answer the phone. She talked to me. And she confessed in part.

"Wendy," she told me, "we are still together."

"But are you sleeping together?"

"We are still together, as much as we were."

"But are you still having *sex?*"

And after a long, careful pause: "We are still together." Always the same words and in the same quiet tone. Patient. Not without empathy. I could hear it in her voice. I could hear that she felt bad. This Other Woman had helped to destroy my marriage. But she offered some real kindness. And at bottom I was somewhat impressed that she was willing to stand in front of me and take my questions, which was more than Bill would do.

I entered into a relationship with Susan that was the perfect illustration of the Stockholm syndrome, in which hostages bond to and even sympathize with the hostage takers. Under that scenario, the hostages are thankful their brains are not blown out and attribute saintliness to the person aiming a gun at them. Provided the trigger is not pulled. It is easy to be grateful that you are not dead. Although of course in many ways, we were. Our marriage was over, though I didn't know it yet. Our home life was destroyed. My boys would soon be waving good-bye to their father on a regular basis as he drove over to the house of his other family.

Much later, I learned several telling details about the affair from Susan's perspective. She told me that when she first met Bill, she was unaware of my existence. He didn't tell her that he was married until much later. Then Bill told her we were separated. Then he told her that we were a union in name only. None of this was true, but it's what she was told. I think she was astonished at my grief, as if she had been programmed all along to expect that I would be nonchalant about her abiding affair with my husband. Her e-mail reads like someone who is not anticipating shock on the receiving end.

But she had a few shocks of her own. Finding out that Bill was married was one. Finding out that we had a second son when she assumed we were separated was another. By the time she had full knowledge of the situation she was deeply in love, unable and, yes, unwilling to extricate herself. She loved Bill. She did not want to leave him. She would not give him up. I asked her incredulously during another phone call, Are you suggesting that we share Bill? She said, Yes. That was fine with her. I hung up, beyond exasperation. I had no idea what to do with that idea or with a woman who could sanction such an arrangement.

There were myriad contacts between the two of us in my hometown, which had also become hers. We would pass in cars on the road. I would see the flash of her hair and my pulse would stop. I saw her get out of Bill's car one afternoon when Bill was supposed to be down in Spring Lake alone with his brother. I saw her cell phone number splashed all over Bill's cell phone when he assured me they were not in touch any longer.

Then one night in late August 2005, Bill refused to come home, again. He said he was spending the night at a hotel. He said he had to figure some things out and did not want to see me just then. When I pressed him for more, he hung up and would not answer his cell phone.

So I called on my parents for babysitting duty and I got into my car. I made the circuit of the hotels in our vicinity until I found Bill's car parked in the garage beneath the Royce Hotel in Brandywine, Pennsylvania. And parked next to it, to my despair, was the Other Woman's car. At least the question of whether they were still having sex had been answered.

An odd digression: In the backseat of Susan's car was a rumple of items—disposable diapers, papers, folded clothing, and a shopping list lying open that I was able to read by squinting. The mind in emotional disarray mimeographs the strangest things. I read that list. I distinctly remember that "escarole" was one of the items on it. I wasn't even clear what you do with escarole. I didn't even know Bill liked it. Oh, if I had only served him escarole for dinner. These are the bizarre and detached details that imprint forever.

I called my little sister from my car phone. In due time she arrived at the hotel with snacks and magazines in case the two of us ended up spending the night in the garage, waiting to shanghai Bill and Susan. That was the initial plan. But we are not patient people. The two of us ended up going inside, intent on finding them. I made up some excuse to the hotel administration that I was worried about Bill, that he wasn't answering his cell phone, and that he had left our house earlier that day distraught. I gave that manager to understand that Bill might hurt himself.

The hotel manager was a deer caught in the headlights. He looked from me to my sister. He hesitated. You could see his mind clicking through the options open to him or perhaps through the role-playing work he had done during job training. He finally looked up the room number and escorted us upstairs, and we three knocked and knocked and knocked on the door of the room, Bill bellowing, "Go away!" from behind it.

I think the truth must have slowly dawned on that manager when I said aloud something about having seen Susan's car parked next to Bill's in the lot downstairs. I am sure the color evaporated from that poor man's face. Oh, the situations he must have seen as a manager at that midlevel hotel. I wonder if the Cornell University School of Hotel Administration provides guidance for this Jerry Springer sort of scenario. It must play itself out in every manager's life on every shift in every hotel all over the world.

My sister and I left that night, having been asked in all politeness to please leave the premises. I did not want to make more trouble for that poor manager. Bill never opened the door, so it was pointless to stand there. But years later, Susan spoke of that night in a phone conversation with me, and she apologized. She said it was agonizing to hear me at the door. She had been terribly conflicted—wanting to answer, wanting to let Bill handle it.

During the labor and delivery of their son, in the summer of 2004, way before I knew, Susan had been given Vioxx to deal with the pain of childbirth. Vioxx was still on the market back then but was shortly to be removed because it was alleged to weaken patients' hearts and cause heart attacks and strokes and blood clots. Susan was one of the victims. She suffered a heart attack on the delivery table, or so Bill told me. She recovered, but she still bears the consequence of it. Her heart was weakened, and for a time one eye was partially closed. Someone I know called this karmic retribution, but I cannot believe it. I would not want that.

Interestingly, several years later, there was an episode of extreme irony when all the agonies came spinning back, but in reverse. I had been out of town for the weekend. It was Sunday morning. I was up in Suffern, New York, in the car with my friend Zane (about whom there will be more later) when I got a frantic call on my cell phone. From Susan. She sounded crazy. She was screaming. She wanted to know, Was I having an affair with Bill?

I think the air around me stopped.

Susan said she had seen Bill at an apartment the night before, walking from the parking lot to the front door with a blonde who looked like me. She said she had been up all night. She had waited outside the apartment all night long for someone to come out. She was crying. Her voice was frayed like unspooling wool. I thought, This is just too bizarre. Beside me, Zane drove the car down I-287, shaking his head at the irony of it all.

My mind went back to that summer phone call in 2005 when I was the one unspooling and Susan took my call. Or that night in the hotel, standing outside of Bill's room, desperate for an answer. I felt I was being directed to remember those incidents for a reason. I held the Other Woman in my hand. It was a responsibility I did not want. There was only one way to answer her: "No," I said. Because it was the truth. Bill later told me he was surprised that I hadn't pretended otherwise, just to torture her. Which tells you most of what you need to know about his adaptive mechanisms.

I stayed on the phone with Susan that morning until she calmed down. I reassured her that the woman she saw had not been me. That I was hours away and had been hours away since Friday night. That Bill had clearly been with someone else. That Bill and I as a couple were dead. I did not ask the obvious: How could she have expected otherwise? This was her business now. Her choice to face.

The Other Woman had become the Woman. And she was teetering on that cliff edge.

Susan in the intervening years has become a somewhat fuller picture for me based on one all-consuming factor: She has been good to my sons. In many ways, she has been a better role model than their father. Many have told me that this is the least she could do. Maybe it is. But I think that is how you see it unless you've been through it, unless you've packed your children's bags and sent them to another home and prayed that they would feel welcome there when the smallest crooked look could ruffle their joy. I just wanted them to be treated kindly. Their vulnerability was temporarily out of my hands.

When Bill moved out of our home in the fall of 2005, he rented an apartment several miles away and lived in it alone. Which is how Susan came to be parked outside of it all night without a key, waiting for a mystery blonde to depart. Eventually, though, as money tightened and then dwindled, Bill moved into Susan's home. That paved the way for my sons to visit their father's other family alto- gether. I packed them off into that void that first afternoon. It killed me to do it. But children need their father, and anyway the courts had divided our time. And so off they went.

They are not Susan's sons, and she does not try to treat them as though they are. At first they did not even know what to call her. The word *mom* is a sacred one and belongs only to me, and *aunt* belongs only to my sister and no one else. They use Susan's last name or something like that. The formality of this arrangement keeps a firm border between them.

There was also this fact: Even before Bill moved out of our home and into his own apartment, and later into a home with

Susan, it became obvious that she really loved my husband. She hadn't wrecked our home for money or for opportunity or for a whim. She really loved Bill. She told me that while Bill and I were married on paper, she and Bill were married by heart. Corny, yes, and self-serving as hell. But I understand the feeling of swept away. Since I have worshipped at that altar my whole life, I couldn't very well repudiate it just because it ran counter to my own needs. I had also been an Other Woman. Understanding came more easily than you might imagine—hard on the heels of fury, yes, but it did come.

Susan's e-mail, which drove me to distraction when I first got it, had ended up making a hard kind of sense. Her enduring affair with my husband was a reality I would simply have to accept. Unless I wanted to burn our whole world down, I would have to find a way to work with it. I did not want to burn our whole world down. I just didn't want my family to break up, so I tried to hold it together for months. It took me a long time to accept the inevitable.

At some point, that acceptance did struggle through the morass of denial and uncertainty. I realized that Susan would not go away, that she would do anything Bill asked, and that he would leave me for her. And that I would have to make peace with the fact of a husband gone for good. The Other Woman, as happens sometimes, ascended, trailing the very burn of karma.

FRIENDS AND FAMILY

IT IS NOT always easy to earn friends. To make them, yes, particularly through the geography of school or neighborhood. Maybe you lean across the aisle in third grade to borrow a pencil from Alison, who is really nice, or you bump into Robert and Zane outside the cafeteria in tenth grade. Maybe you live next door to the Watsons, whose mother tolerates endless raidings of cabinets. Maybe the woman who gives you piano lessons has a daughter and you befriend her over a shared annoyance with the metronome. These are the most carefree alliances. You owe them to the classroom seating chart or the street your parents bought a house on.

But earned friendships are something else. Those are the ones that arise out of no particular commonality. They have the shimmer of being almost fated, since their discovery is due entirely to chance. To keep these friendships you have to earn their presence in your life, until they have a solid purchase there and can breathe on their own.

I have had some perfect earned friendships over the years—a woman named Carol Braha who spontaneously called me from California after reading a story I wrote for the *New York Times*; a man named Rikki whom I met on the street in Boston after I dropped my roses and he picked them up; and a group of women I came to know in 1988 when I was out with Tommy, named by Tommy's brother and known ingloriously as the Hens. That is when I began to cement earned friendships with a flock of women who would alternately influence and endure the whip end of my adultery. I am lucky they are with me still.

I met Tommy because I was out in my hometown with these women, celebrating Sarah's coming marriage to Tommy's brother. At the time, I had known Sarah for many years but not well or deeply. I knew Jean hardly at all. I met the others—Babs, Annie, Andrea—only that night. Sarah's family ran an art and camera supply shop in town that had a devoted following of pacifists and vegetarians and glamorous hippies. I visited Sarah there often, where Jean worked as well. The more I patronized that store, the more I returned and leaned over the glass countertop to talk, the more something began to take shape. It was incipient friendship, arising over tubes of paint and camera batteries and cropped photographs. I was invited to the pub in Brandywine with them that summer night in 1988. And everything took off from there.

At the time, I was the only Hen who was married. Babs was newly divorced. Jean was soon to meet her husband. Sarah was engaged. Annie was in love. Andrea was looking with a caustic sort of swagger for the next man. I found my marital status inconvenient to the life they were leading. Not that they found it inconvenient. I did. I wanted to be out—with the Hens, with Tommy, in the night, in the summer. It was all of a piece, and whether one was the greater influence on the other I can't exactly say.

Beginning with Tommy's affair and over the years after, I dragged the Hens and many others into the oil slick of my infidelity. In varying degrees they were all tarnished. It would be near impossible to keep family and friends out of the spill grid. Separated from their tribe, elephants can die of loneliness. I found the conduct of affairs enough of a strain without also trying to keep them secret from those closest to me.

In the past, I have wondered what kind of toll this took on them, what it did to their sense of morality for me to force my infidelity on them. To expose them to my excuses and alibis. If I was out with a man, all Bill knew was that I was out with a friend. Or a group of people, which almost always meant the Hens plus one. It wasn't until I got a phone call one night more recently from my friend Aidan that I realized just how much of a burden a friend's adultery isn't and is.

I could hear it in Aidan's voice that night, the overweening desire to tell. There was such excitement in his tone, and real suffering already. He was calling to tell me he had met someone at a professional conclave in New York City a few weeks before. She was all he could think about. The two of them had sat talking at the table long after the evening wound down. Then they had moved to another bar and sat there. Then they had talked into the night and mostly through it. They had experienced more compatibility in one evening than he had felt with his wife in years, he told me. This was not a good sign.

It was all there, everything that I recognized from my own reaction to another person's allure. The desire to dive in. The thrill of meeting someone you cannot stop thinking about. The urgency to see that person again. The anxiety of waiting, the mind already grinding away on the obstacles to be overcome. How quickly you rise to duplicity. How quickly you can't stand the thought of the spouse alone at home, less and less wanted.

Two weekends later, Aidan and this woman would reunite. She lived in another state and was flying in to meet him. I knew all the details. I had been given phone numbers and hotel locations and an outline of the plans, just in case. And although I was not asked to participate in the execution of these plans, my whole weekend was shot through with an awareness of the two of them in motion. I wondered if they had met at the airport without incident. I wondered if they had gone straight to the hotel as planned. I wondered if Aidan's wife called him or if she assumed he was where he said he would be. I imagined them sharing their first kiss, their first moments in bed, their first awareness of the misery they would engender.

I couldn't get them out of my mind. I felt not exactly guilty, but something like guilt. And I was so worried. Agitated, almost. I knew there would be moments when Aidan and his woman would dissolve into sex or adoration and thus be oblivious to the stress of an affair. But me, I was on full alert the whole weekend.

Is this how the Hens felt all those years ago? It is terrible. It is a serious obligation. Your knowledge not only makes you complicit, it makes you drunk with concern. I worried about something going wrong. I worried about getting a phone call from Aidan's wife. I worried about whether I would be called upon to lie on someone else's behalf.

Of course, you receive not only the burden of alibis but the breathless phone call afterward, heavy with detail. I got Aidan's call after that first weekend, telling me he was crazy about her. That sex had been everything he had hoped for. That their conversation had proven how well suited they were. He didn't want to go home. He was sitting in his car two miles away on the side of the road, dreading the thought of his wife. Dreading. It was difficult for me to know how to feel, or to feel only one way. He sounded so happy. And so miserable. What is there to say to such folly? I mostly just listened.

Their affair continued for months. Finally they decided that Aidan would leave his wife (his girlfriend wasn't married, and there were no children on either side). He wasn't in love with his wife anymore, maybe never had been. He had met someone else who moved him more, too much more to go back home and accept a marriage gone cold. That is his business and his life. But I see where someone with knowledge of an affair is squeezed into a corner. Every principle is called into play, including and most especially loyalty. The question is, loyalty to whom?

As I saw it, my loyalty was to my friend. I would never have turned my back on him. I would never have gone to his wife. I did not see that as my place. What was my place? To sit in the front row of that theater performance, wait to see if it turned into a comedy or a tragedy, and make sure the lights didn't come on too early in the house behind me. To wait in anxious patience while they decided what was best for their lives.

I was asked at the time, Would you tell Aidan's wife? Would you tell if it were someone else? Would you tell if it were your brother-in-law betraying your sister? Your best friend's husband betraying your best friend? Your father betraying your mother? I hate these kinds of questions. They are fair, but there is never a straight answer. Perhaps some people think there should be, but I am not one of them.

Suppose I went to Aidan's wife. Suppose I told her. Suppose she flipped out and got into her car. And drove off and had an accident. And was killed. Or never came home. Or registered for ownership of a gun. Or left Aidan instantly and without any discussion and took the whole marriage down. Who am I to force this consequence on him or on them? Aidan and his family have to live with the fallout of his behavior and his choices, not me. If the consequences were mine, I might feel differently. But largely I thought, No. I would not tell in most situations.

If it were my sister being betrayed, my mother, my best friend, I would go to the betrayer first. I would say, What do you plan to do about this now that I know? I would say, The jig is up and now you have to make a decision and you'd better make it quickly or I will have to make it for you. I would not bring down the whole marriage without trying first to see if there is something else to be done. I would take that position not because I have been on the side of betrayal, but because I see my responsibility to my friends and my family in a larger light. And because I don't think an affair needs always to wreck a marriage. If that can be avoided, it should be.

The back-and-forth strangeness of all this wraps itself around a night two years before, in 2004, when I was having dinner with two of the Hens at the Temperance House. It was just before Christmas and we were talking about New Year's resolutions. I remember quite clearly telling them that I planned to be a better wife in the coming year. That I had been neglectful of Bill, that I favored my sons' company over his, that we no longer had the close union we were capable of. I remember feeling a surge of warmth for my husband. I visualized the couple we could become in 2005. I couldn't wait to start. I would start that very night.

But it was already too late in the game. I was to find out four weeks from that night that Bill had a mistress and a new baby in the world who bore his name. One of these friends would be walking through my front door and I would be dreading Chechnyan separatists. Both of the women sitting at that tavern with me knew it was coming. All those years of bearing the brunt of my infidelities had reversed the course of the stream, and now they were faced with telling me about Bill and Susan and their child.

I wonder if they looked at each other over the dinner plates and glasses at the tavern that night, if some quick glance acknowledging the lousy job ahead of them was exchanged. I noticed nothing. Behind the scenes, things were developing quickly. One friend had recently visited the county courthouse, looking up deeds to see whose name was on the house in which Susan lived and to see who had purchased it. Others had been inquiring about Bill and his association with Susan. They had been doing this for two months, just to be sure of the outline before they came to me. Just to be sure they weren't wrong. They held out for that possibility. You see movies about this stuff: people trying to figure out what to do, how to do it, how to tell someone something terrible. Even while they hope it is not true. But I had to be told. When there is a child in the mix, well, that's game over.

As weird fate would have it, my former lover Terry had a hand in this, too. He had been told about Susan by a mutual friend who had a neighbor who had a friend who knew someone who lived across the street from her, et cetera et cetera. A huge scaffolding of associations gets constructed around us just by living our lives. When the news is grim, it condenses down to a small, hard ball, like obsidian, and gets passed along carefully from one to another until someone has to set it down. Terry was that someone.

After our affair ended, Terry and I had loosely remained friends. We kept track of each other. We knew many of the same people. Terry was a good man, but a long way from his own path at that point. I did not want to lose sight of him. I have never found it easy to give up someone I have loved and always sought to keep relationships in some form or other. We became natural friends, and that was enough. But by 2004, the obsidian ball had passed to him, and he was obliged to do something with it.

Over the two months preceding Christmas, Terry was in touch with the Hens, first to let them know about Bill and Susan and after that to figure out what to do. He wanted to tell me about Bill sooner rather than later. The others insisted we wait. Just until after Christmas, Terry was told. Just let them have Christmas. All of this went on in hushed phone calls and urgent visits. My friends circled around behind me, anxious and deliberating but galvanized. When I think of this, and the price I exacted for my own infidelities, I do shudder.

I do not know how it goes with other people. But I was backed and supported continually, even and especially when the situation was bad. When I was cheating on Bill and when he was cheating on me, many people knew. Friends and family form the circle of the silent, complicit minority camped around the fact of betrayal. I am sure Bill and Susan had such a circle, pierced only in the late months of 2004. They must have. Pregnancy is obvious. There are always people who know a lot more than the spouse.

There is a blast radius to bad news. Once the story of Bill and Susan was out in the open in early 2005, it was hard for friends and family to know what to say to me. I was surprised by the unevenness of the counsel I was given. Those I had always considered the wisest suddenly had the least to say. Those I thought would have nothing to say suddenly waxed brilliant. The garage mechanic rivaled the longtime friend in terms of solace. Counsel and support came from the most unexpected places. Some people were simply curious, others were brimming with compassion. I got a phone call from the father of a childhood friend, a formidable, stern man who had lived across the street from us and who had always terrified me as a kid even though I liked him. He called me and said, "Tough times, huh?" and didn't hang up even when I started to cry. You cannot predict the kindness you will receive. It is so welcome that it hurts.

I always hated it, though, when the advice was cheap. It's all right to have no answer. It's not all right to conjure one out of no-where just to fill up the void or so you can hear the salacious details. I was told to stick with Bill or we would be destitute. I was told to leave him by people who would climb back into their cars and drive gratefully home to their happy families. I was told by a neighbor who had never befriended me but who knew what was going on, "Well, after all, there are ups and downs in life." Yes, and please do go hang yourself on your own banal pronouncements. Better yet, do not speak.

I was counseled to "take all the money!" and "destroy Bill!" and "I would kill him!" and "I would take the children away!" I al-ways wanted to say, No, I don't think that is how you would handle it. Perhaps you think you would. More than likely, you would not. And legally, you cannot. Those are just easy words to say. Real advice, good advice, is much harder.

As for my family, this preternaturally opinionated tribe, the re-actions were admirable. Bill wasn't written off, not immediately. It wasn't the worst story anyone in our broader family had ever gener-ated. We have our share of drug arrests and lithium-addled cousins and alcoholics at the dinner table. But I think it may have been the strangest story. I know the effects of Bill's affair rippled out in every direction. I know my cousins joined ranks behind me. I know some family members told Bill to stop showing up at our regular vacation beach spot in Ocean City, New Jersey, with Susan and his baby in tow. I know my mother planned—and does still—to have a word or two with Susan should she ever run into her.

But I suppose the best reaction came from my niece Kessey. She made me laugh. She had just found out about Bill and Susan and sent a cogent e-mail from college. It was slugged, "What the fuck?!" I'm not sure anyone—therapist or friend, paid or called in the middle of the night, my side or his—summed up the situation any better than that.

But some reactions were unwelcome. My uncle, the one at Christmas, the one who cannot countenance women in the military, sent me a letter in which he explained in almost prideful detail the likelihood that men will cheat on their spouses. Whereas women will not. He pinned it all on biology.

It was not surprising that this boys-will-be-boys defense arose from such a source. It is a thin and predictable argument. I was forced to write a letter of my own to my uncle in which I told him how deeply wrong his theory was. I admitted that I had had affairs as well as Bill, which fact my uncle had not previously known. I admitted that I knew more women who had cheated than men who had cheated. I volunteered he should keep his antiquated notions of male seed spreading the hell away from me.

The received certainty that men cheat more than women doesn't sit well. I just do not think it's true. There are not men who cheat and women who endure them. There are people who cheat and there are people who don't. It divides much more neatly along those lines. Spouses weaken at the same rate, as the (male) poet Galway Kinnell puts it. Look at Madame Bovary. Look at Anna

Karenina. It's only literature, but it's great literature, and nothing if not reflective of our humanity. I raised myself on these classics, which may have been where I got the idea in the first place. They examine the adultery of wives. Men have thousands of studies focusing on their betrayal. But we have Flaubert and Tolstoy.

The fallout, too, seems impervious to gender. Not long ago a friend of mine spent the night in a hotel room, which is sometimes what you do when you find out your spouse has been having a year-long affair. His flight was sadly predictable—it's all many of us are capable of after discovering such a betrayal—though I am sure he realizes now that mere movement is not a fix for that kind of agony.

My friend Zane and I were sitting with him at coffee one morning, listening to him talk. He was red-eyed and spent and manic, having been up all night reading the sex-drenched e-mails his wife had sent her lover. I recognized this behavior. There is a necessity to know everything. You have been kept so utterly in the dark that you suddenly want to hear every excruciating detail, to fit it all together. This has something to do with processing and acceptance. But that's not how it feels at the time. It feels like a compulsion. Which is why you stay up all night reading about your wife's favorite sexual position with her new lover.

The point is, my friend is a man. He is a man, but he acted exactly the way I had acted. Crazed. Unbelieving. Self-torturing. Laughing maniacally one minute, talking of normal things a moment later, raging the one after that. Most spouses behave this way. It does not matter whether you're a man or a woman when it comes to ground zero. If you're standing there, gender recedes and all kinds of maladjusted behaviors come tromping along like camp followers. We all break in the same human way.

For ten months throughout 2005, I received serious life support from my family and friends. They rallied around our troubled house from the end of January to the end of October. The very closest of them took a position that seems to me more helpful than anything. A position that I would like to pass on now that the egg white has passed through the eggshell and I can see the wisdom of it.

Of those friends and family members closest to me, only one or two of them told me I should leave Bill. I am sure they all thought it. I am sure most of them wanted to strangle him or steal the boys and me away for our own good. It was hard on them to watch the dissolution. It was particularly hard for my parents. One night in late February, I called them after discovering a cache of X-rated photographs from Bill and Susan's affair stored on our family computer. In response to my anguished phone call, my parents sped over in their car. But not until after my father had pulled over to the side of the road, rolled down his window, and gotten violently sick out of it. He was seventy-one years old at the time.

During the worst of it, my parents lost weight and stopped sleeping. I think they each aged terribly under the strain. Given their lives up to that point—lucky, cosseted—they had few skills to use against this raft of horrors. My father blames himself to this day for not taking Bill out to the woodpile and thrashing him senseless. It is testimony to their decency, then, that these closest people never shouted at me to leave. In fact, whatever I said Bill and I were going to do was supported. I may have been nodded at like an idiot, but I wasn't aware of any condescension. I think everyone realized the marriage would end and they simply waited for me to realize it, too.

Depending on who is going through them, separation and divorce have their own geologic ages. For some people those are short and cataclysmic, the whole mess roiling the global weather and then blowing out in a matter of weeks or months. It was that way for my friend who had read his wife's e-mails. He recovered and divorced fairly quickly and is now living quite happily with another woman.

For others, like me, the recovery takes forever. I went through ages of despair and ages of hope. Bill kept changing his mind and his address. He rented an apartment in the fall of 2005 into which he disappeared regularly. But he kept coming back home, too. And each time he did, I exhaled with relief. And friends and family could do little but stand at the gates of the fort and let one spouse or the other out and then back in again depending on the time of day.

You are never ready to do something until you are ready to do something. Regardless of how many fingerprints there are on your back from those pushing you forward, you will balk at the edge until you decide to jump. This is so obvious that it hardly needs saying. But a friend who is suffering through a bad situation is unable to end it until that precise moment when his or her own clarity steals forward. Patience is an essential quality of friendship until then.

During those months, I was often asked why I wanted to stay with Bill. Not as a judgment. More as a test. To see if my thinking on the matter was still sound. It was. I loved Bill. I couldn't imagine not having him as a husband and father. I didn't want my family ruptured. I invested heavily in radical hope: the idea that something miraculous could arise out of miraculous effort. Stupid effort, as it turns out.

It was at about this time that two of my best friends from high school came back into my life and, alongside the Hens, joined the Wendy Plump Council in Support of Hopeless Causes. They had been on the perimeter for decades. But our friendships resumed with vigor that summer owing to everyone's weird situations.

Robert and Zane. They had grown up in the same neighborhood about fifteen minutes from my own. They were boyhood friends. The three of us had, in fact, bumped into one another outside that school cafeteria when we were in tenth grade. That moment hangs in my mind like something out of *National Geographic*, the three of us beholding one another as we would members of a bizarre new tribe. As, at the time, we were. I was a young woman. They were young men. To one another we were as exotic as Yanomami warriors. But we became friends and we stayed friends straight through the rest of high school, through separate college careers, through separate marriages and adult lives.

Robert married early. His three children were born before my first, but his separation came about a year earlier than my own. His wife had already asked him to move out in 2004. He was well into the ninth circle of hell when I started down to meet him there. He used to come over to my house in the afternoons before I knew about Bill and Susan, and he would sit next to the hammock while I rocked my youngest son—just home from kindergarten—to sleep in it.

Later, much later, I had this great idea to set Robert up with a single woman I knew named Michelle. Robert and Michelle married in 2010.

And then there was Zane. Zane lived with his grown son in northern New Jersey near his ex-wife, so we rarely saw him. I kept up on his life through phone calls and other people's sightings—someone had seen Zane windsurfing at the Jersey shore, heard about Zane moving into a research and design position, seen Zane raising his son, known Zane after his own divorce when he was dating a schoolteacher, a psychologist, a wing nut.

He got a bleak phone call from me at his home one night during the summer of 2005. I was crying. I asked him, How do I do this? Zane had already been through a divorce, the only person I knew well enough at the time to ask. I wanted him to hand me the primer for the equation. I wanted a way out. And I wanted someone who had already passed through it to deed me the code. I don't remember what Zane said to me that night. I do know he was in the middle of a cycling workout and stopped in order to hear me—which, knowing now the compulsive nature of Zane's athleticism, is saying a lot. I also know he relived through the grief of my crumbling marriage every moment of his own, even though it had already been over five years for him.

By the end of October, it became obvious even to me that my marriage was finished for good. I had fought against it every step of the way. Eventually, though, things do fall out the way they're going to fall out. Eventually you are ready to throw up your hands.

My youngest son had always had attacks of croup. Occasionally he woke up at night unable to breathe. On this particular night, he woke up wheezing. Bill and I hustled him outside as usual, into the colder air. But he was still laboring a bit. I wanted to take him to the hospital rather than wait for the croup to abate because I was scared. I didn't want it to worsen. I would drive to the hospital alone with him while Bill stayed home with our oldest boy, still asleep upstairs.

We got ready to go quickly. However, as we were throwing things together I realized that my cell phone was dead. It had no juice. It did not even switch on. I didn't want to drive to the emergency room without a way to reach someone in case my son's breathing deteriorated. I needed Bill's phone. I turned to Bill and asked for it. Where is your phone, I said, I need it for the drive. Bill hesitated. Then looked away from me. He would not give it to me. For days he had been telling me that he was no longer in touch with Susan, that they had not spoken in weeks, that he was home with me for good. No doubt his cell phone would have shown otherwise.

I remember watching for half a moment his awkward, fumbling attempts to plug in my cell phone and load enough juice over the next five seconds for my drive to the emergency room. I remember a feeling of disgust, watching him flounder around. I had to leave. I couldn't wait.

I put my son in his car seat and climbed behind the wheel. Just before I drove off, with no cell phone, I locked eyes with Bill. Everything seemed to slide into slow motion. This is the way it is when some terrible accident is befalling you—car crash, plunge off a cliff, end of a marriage. I looked hard at Bill. I felt I was seeing him clearly for the first time and for the first time was aware of the perverse depth of his secrets and the extent to which he would go to protect them. It was the absolute moment when I knew my marriage was over.

The next day, when my son and I were home safely from the hospital, I called my friends and family to tell them the news. Bill had moved out for good. I had not asked him to go. He went on his own. He packed another bag and he split. Again. I don't remember the moment all that clearly. What I do remember is sitting the night before in the emergency room, holding my youngest son in my arms while he slept. I was thinking, There is no way we can come back from this. Risk my faith in you, I can deal. Risk my son's safety, I cannot. We had been married for eighteen years. Infidelity ran a drunken course through many of them. This was its graceless terminus.

I have had friends approach me over the years about adultery. Even people I don't know well would say, I think I am going to have an affair; what should I do? At times I have felt like the infidelity czar, not exactly the role I envisioned for myself as a young woman. But it's a serious question. It seems to bedevil most people at some point in their marriages. The answer is never clear. People seek out other partners for reasons of their own, and some of those are good reasons.

I wouldn't take responsibility for a definitive answer on something so complicated and irreversible. I do not think you can tell someone what to do in the very biggest matters. What I do, though, is point to my own marriage and how poorly it has gone for me and for Bill. I tell them not all marriages that sustain adultery need to be trashed, and I believe that to this day. There is a lot lost in trust, but it is a smaller scope of loss than you will endure with a divorce. And the family gets to stay a family.

My own marriage, though, was ruined by it. The affairs metastasized in our relationship from the inside out. By the time all that infidelity was said and done, there was little left to save. Our marriage had become like a leaf eaten away by caterpillars, where the petiole and midrib remain with some ghostly connective tracery in between. Not enough to hold a drop of rain. And it was called upon to hold so much more. Little boys. A home. Love. Memory.

I don't know that infidelity was the only thing that tanked our marriage or that we would still be together without it. But for my own part, I suspect we would have been. Marriage is more than a question of monogamy. I realize this is a convenient position for one such as myself. But there is a lot to consider in the union of two people. There are many large vows taken on a wedding day. There are vows about sickness and health and richer and poorer and that one about death doing us part. That was the vow I cherished most when I married Bill. It was the one I swore to. I meant to bear him company straight through old age.

Once Bill left, I fell back again on family and friends to handle the coming weeks and months without him. I visited with them more. I arranged playdates for my sons like mad. I kept a steady hum in the household, a white noise that would drown out the absence. My sons and I stopped eating in the kitchen and ate instead in the living room, where we would talk or I would read aloud through their dinner. It was a cozier way to have a meal, without Bill's seat aggressively empty before us. We got through a library of books that fall and winter—*Eragon, Half Magic, Gregor, Freddy Goes to Florida*, and the great French children's story *Nicholas*, books one, two, and three.

I knew that I would still need men around and in my life. So I talked with Robert every day or he came over every day. I was invited to a U2 concert with Zane that would take place several months later. I went cycling with another male friend of mine, and his deep, rough voice exhorted me up the biggest hills. They were my fix. It would be a nice little life, I thought. Raise my sons. Hang with my friends. Be a good mother, a good sister, a good daughter. And when I wanted or needed male companionship, I would turn chastely to my male friends. Just for the atavistic kick of deep voices, rough physiques, large hands. The world of men, which I had always loved, which I would need now to import. That is how I planned to live.

A few days after Bill moved out, Jean called an emergency dinner of the Hens at her house. She circled the wagons. There was comfort food and the familiar rhythm of her grandfather clock in the doorway. There was a disco ball that someone found in her basement and switched on. There was mood-appropriate music, which could only mean Van Morrison. There was the comfort of familiar voices. The comfort of Hens.

Our children were in the background, playing among themselves, growing up en masse like a litter. For that moment, but only for that moment, everything was fine. Over the years, friendship is called upon to have many kinds of strengths. It is bent and recast in different degrees depending on the situation. It has to remain loose as water for joy and the lesser dramas and instantly convert to graphite for the most serious. I think I have paced my relationships through every kind of field test and found them durable and sound.

I bless the tensile strength of friends.

STORMING THE SANCTUARY

NFIDELITY ISN'T THE Orkney Islands. It's not Vanuatu. It's not foreign and exotic. It is shared, well-trammeled terrain. It's the Jersey shore. It's Orlando, Windsor Castle, the Eiffel Tower. Not everyone has visited, but everyone is acquainted with the destination. Infidelity is somewhere most married people have been, if not in person, then as armchair travelers. Movies have taken us there and books, news, history, politics, the lives of movie stars. We've been there through a cousin's experience or a neighbor's or a friend's, or our own. It's common, very common. It's the corner store at the end of the street.

But it has the allure of Vanuatu.

Once you go there, it is very difficult to come back home again whole. The reentry will kill off some small part of you that will not regenerate. Knowing this, I should be able to say with unparalleled conviction that the travel is not worth the price. But I can't. I can only say that with a three-quarter heart, the other quarter casting toward the allure, fully aware that there is lasting power in that, too.

Infidelity is a siren call. It offers up a seduction of enticements that is difficult for some to deny. Passion, sex, discovery, romance, the chance to be adored anew, the chance to be somewhere else while that somewhere else is all aglitter. It makes the marital home seem lackluster, even drab. I have paid richly in order to remain in that temporary, other world. And so has Bill.

But infidelity in itself is not a different place from the one most of us initially visit when we fall in love. Dramatically speaking, most people get to that state in the very beginning with those who will become spouses or partners. We have been to that country before it was an illegal entry. We had to have been there. Otherwise we would not have made the choice to marry.

I had been there with Bill for several years in the very beginning. Apart from the obvious moral transgressions, I did not find the attractions of my adulterous lovers inherently different from the early stages of falling in love with Bill. There was nothing about the risk of infidelity, of getting caught, that made it more attractive to me. In fact, that made it much worse because deceit was factored in.

I simply loved falling in love. It was a gorgeous country. I found it to be the most alluring destination of all. I did not plan to leave. I do not know how I slipped out of its borders apart from the daily drift of months and years together with Bill. With adultery you get to go back to that place again when perhaps your life has already established itself in some less glamorous corner. You get to visit the mountain villages of Gstaad while you're living in some suburb of Philadelphia.

I have made so many choices in my life that were almost by default. They may have been the best choices at the time, but they still committed a price I was a bit clueless about when I made them: spouses or partners, children, homes, jobs, shared friends, a shared community. These arise naturally out of two people coming together.

They are a form of bedrock and they anchor you, which is always a mercy if you can appreciate it. Still, much of the allure dissipates over that ground, like fog burning off. Adultery brings it back.

I remember a skiing vacation in Vermont I took with my family when I was a little girl, maybe ten years old. I was looking out of my bedroom window at night at the snow outside spangled by the klieg lights of the ski village. At the sweet wood smoke coming out of the chimneys. At the movement of people inside those condos. At the snowy boots left outside and the skis, still crusty with snow from the last run, stacked against the snowdrifts. I was well enclosed within that circle of comfort. It was all very snug.

But in the distance, behind all of that habitation, were the mountains. They looked so blue and cold and forbidding. So indifferent to the village where I stood looking out the window. One view was such a contrast to the other, and that focused my interest at first. But that image of the mountains is what lasts for me. I wanted to go there. I wanted to put on my boots and walk out of the well-lit house and be lost in that world. It was a strong and bewildering temptation.

Allure is a difficult place to resist at any age. The long married know this. There is a price to pay for monogamy. You make the choice to be with one person, and then you discover that what you had been hearing from the older and wiser had all along been true. The passion does fade. The attraction abates. The mystery becomes too daily. Committed life subsides into something comfortable. Particularly when you are younger, it is difficult to stack it next to the presenting magic of a new relationship and have it compare favorably. You do not think of comfort as a muse. You believe that comfort is boring. You miss the fire. If you are foolhardy or just nostalgic;

if you are lonely or if you are disappointed; if you are bored or if you are restless; if you are me or if you are like me: You go in search of some other destination.

And so I did. I had imagined I was finished with adultery once I became a mother. I have said that it was not risk that I craved in my liaisons. Obviously there were elements of risk to the marriage, but I did not seek out adultery for the thrill of risk. And I did not dwell on the risk of my behavior while I was newly married and did not yet have children. But once my first son was born, and then my second, the idea of being one of those parents hiding in a hotel room with a person not your spouse became sordid. I did not want to be that person.

I do remember, though, being in a café in Princeton one morning with my two young sons. We were sipping orange juice and eating muffins. I felt lethargic, exhausted. My sons and I were sitting next to a Princeton professor and her young charge, a student obviously in the Program in Women and Gender Studies who was listing ideas for her thesis project. The drift of her ideas was killing me. She wanted to do something about Catholic nine morality as it was foisted on the Irish peasantry in the early nineteenth century. Or should it be earlier? she asked. Should it be the sixteenth century or sometime during the Dark Ages? Perhaps instead of Ireland it should be France or Great Britain or the women met by postslavery missionaries in equatorial Africa. I wanted to lean over the table and ask her, Could you choose something closer to home? Maybe her thesis could yield some answers to the bewildering task of new motherhood.

I had not intended to be derailed by infidelity again. Well, I was. Shortly after that episode of orange juice and lethargy, an old, well-known voice came calling—allure in the form of Declan. I had met Declan in Boston years before when I lived there right after college. We went boating in Newport and were nearly run over by a container ship. He showed up outside my apartment one night, calling up from the street. We spent a day in Woods Hole, driving out from the city with champagne and crackers. "Do you travel with your passport?" he asked me that afternoon. I gave up resisting anything at that point.

When I lived in Boston, I didn't have high school or parents or college responsibilities to get in the way. I was an adult and every call was my own. Boston was a good place for that sort of thing. It was full to crazy with young men and women just like me. Sprung for the first time. Into that thick heat of youth Declan sauntered, confident and funny and brash as hell. He loved to talk and he loved to argue, and he was good at both. We could sit for hours listening to each other's takes on life. We were cocksure young philistines, thoroughly untested. But since this was true of both of us, it went unnoticed at the time. It was enough that we shared our little philosophies with each other.

Declan has always been one of those people who got away, meaning that the timing was never right between us. I was in love with Bill, or Declan was in love with someone. The planets were not aligned, and we never fell into a relationship. There are people whom you might have loved and did not get to, and they linger in your mind as cast-off pieces of kindling for you to strike yourself against later in life. He ghosted the more poignant moments of my regret, hanging over them, whispering, *You should have! You should have!* I always thought there would be more time to decide about him.

Declan called me during the summer of 2001 to say he would be coming to Philadelphia for an event with his company in late August. He wanted to see me. He wondered if I could get away to meet him. Knowing full well what he was asking and what I was agreeing to, I said yes. I had two beautiful children, a good home, a decent marriage so far as I knew (though by this point Bill had already been with Susan for nearly six years). All the same, I have to admit I did not hesitate. I took the bait. I stormed my own sanctuary.

Why did I do it? Anything I say will sound like an excuse of the kind I, and then Bill, used many years before in the therapist's office. And yet to a degree they are all true. I was bored. I was not an interesting point of study, the way a nineteenth-century Irish Catholic peasant apparently was. I missed passion. I had two young boys, and I felt about as sexy as a hatchback. Something had gone out of our marriage. But there was another reason. It was a simple one. I have mentioned it before. I just wanted.

It is a well-traveled observation that people come to resemble their dogs. It can be the same with spouses. Through years of co-habitation, the gender differences break down. The wife starts taking out the trash and grouting the bathroom tile and builds a fire; the husband rocks the baby to sleep and cooks a holiday dinner and stops on the way home from work to buy tampons for the women in his family. All of this is necessary to running a smooth household. But it's not always conducive to great sex.

Sex is rarely bad. Or I am lucky to say that, for me, it has not been. It has run aground on boredom once or twice. But it has not been bad, even after years of marriage. Still, you need to be reminded of how cool it is to be a woman or to be a man. To have an affair is to be plunged back into the pool of your own gender. It is a full-immersion reminder of how strong men are, how soft a woman's body is, how good it feels to have someone's weight slowly lowering onto you, how men sound, how men taste, and how beautifully you can deal with these senses as a woman inspired. These are things that get away from you during a long relationship.

I wanted a night of tender appraisal. I wanted to feel desire and to be desired again. I wanted the oblivion of sex. I wanted to be with Declan, who in my convenient view should have been grandfathered into my marital contract since he was well lodged in my life long before there was a contract. I knew it was wrong. But wrong was once again less important than want.

So I made up an excuse to be away for the night. Years of practicing this kind of behavior rushed back to me. I had a host of proven, well-worn excuses to choose from, some of them provided by my husband. I was out with a bunch of people. I drove around all night smoking a cigar. I need some downtime in Atlantic City. I need to do a story in Florida. I had to leave Thanksgiving dinner to get my book. I am going to Russia. I will not go to the Jersey shore with you. I am leaving for Mississippi. I am going shark fishing in South Carolina. My phone doesn't work. My recharge is lost. My hotel room is locked and you may not enter. I am going to Spring Lake for the day with my brother.

I used whatever alibi would fit. And then I went to Philadelphia.

Would it be disappointing to say otherwise—because it was an astonishing night. Declan was brilliant. He was brilliant and loving and passionate. When I first walked up to him in the hotel lobby and put my arms around his neck to hug him, he was shaking. He was atremble. It was a powerful moment, the first glimpse in a decade of someone I might have been happier with.

After dinner, back at the hotel, we went up to Declan's room. I loved the smell of him. I loved the feel of his hands on me. I loved the sound of this different, deeper male voice next to me in bed. I loved the shower we took and the way he pushed all my wet hair back off my face for a full-on view. There was no hiding behind lots of blond that night. I felt a complete woman. It was the most intimate night of romance I had had in years. I came so close to crossing the border of someone else. It seemed worth it to be back in that place, that sweet dislocation of Vanuatu.

We stayed at the suite in Declan's hotel, the white marble façade of Philadelphia's City Hall lit up just across the street. I woke up before dawn knowing exactly where I was, hearing a foreign rhythm of breathing beside me. Lovers look beautiful when they are sleeping. I watched Declan for a long time. All the questions of what we might have been assembled in that room with us, giving the scene its own sad dignity. Outside the window, the City Hall clock face loomed large and yellow, like that clock Peter Pan lands on in the Walt Disney movie. I woke Declan up to point it out to him. It was a precious moment. And despite the wreck I was sure to become after, I was grateful for all of it. He was the last, most poignant affair.

A week later, a package arrived in the mail for me at my home. It was a milk mug that Declan had found somewhere. It was emblazoned with the image of Peter Pan flying past the clock tower, trailing a golden scatter of pixie dust. And a week after that was September 11, which with its trauma and fallout swept away ambition for anything more than the comfort of home and family. I have not seen Declan since.

Still, I lament marriage. It is not the fault of marriage that it pales. But it does. Boredom can pull you out of your chosen orbit, particularly the domestic orbit. Like alcohol or drug abuse or gambling or depression, adultery is simply one of the five forces of disorder. It's the only one, though, without a Twelve-Step Program to help strangle the allure. So marriage keeps getting choked by it.

I know of so many instances of adultery just among my own acquaintances. Some rival the disaster that mine proved to be; some were just banal. None of them came off well. Adultery never ends well. Even in the least dramatic cases, even in the ones that are resolved smoothly, there follows a period of smash.

One of my favorite anti-stories involves the friend of a friend. Call her Nancy. Nancy was about as severe toward the idea of infidelity as a person could be. She roundly condemned it at every opportunity. In her mind there was never an excuse for it. Never, ever. She sounded a little like one of those televangelists spewing hell and damnation at the rest of us for behavior they are later found to be committing on a regular basis. She telegraphed that impression for good reason.

When Nancy went away for a vacation with this friend of mine, she met a man. She fell for him, hard. She came home to her family five days later a wet wreck, wanting little more than to be with her lover. Of course. You are sick with longing. I understand this. I don't judge her for it. In the end, though, Nancy left her husband and her daughter to run off with her lover. Like any rapid convert, she did not hesitate to blow the whole ship out of the water. She is with her lover still, many years later. So the attraction had some solidity to it after all. But in my eyes she is unrecognizable to the person she had been previously. This is what irks me. I do wish people would acknowledge the possibility of a gray area before they have some personal stake in it.

That is simply one story among many that I know. A girlfriend of mine once called me to ask that I come over and get her drunken husband's mistress out of her home. He had brought the woman home to meet his wife, so addled in drink that he saw no reason why the two of them shouldn't immediately hit it off. Of course, I was more than happy to clear her out.

I know of someone else who fell in love with a woman and was preparing to leave his family for her. His family was told, and they were devastated. Nevertheless, he prepared to go. On the eve of his departure, his lover was killed in a car crash. Unable to deal with the tragedy alone, this man crawled back home to his wife and children. They took him in and he lives there still.

I know of someone else who left her husband and three sons for another man. Just split. She met someone and off she went, and all those previous men were left to deal as best they could without a wife and mother. She lived down the road from my house. I used to drive by that forlorn home, witness to its increasing deterioration. It came to look exactly like what it was. Abandoned.

I know of someone else whose husband cheated, left, then came home again. He is living with his ex-wife as a kind of organic roommate, and not just for the sake of finances. The kids have both their parents under one roof. She has someone new. He has someone new. The four of them even go out to dinner together. It would never do for me, but it works for them. I am curious, though, about how they split the cost of the meal.

I know lots of people who congratulate themselves on never having cheated but who nevertheless engage in all sorts of nonpenetrative behavior. Watercooler affairs. E-mail affairs, Twitter relationships, cell phone lovers. They're not exactly betrayal. But they're not exactly cool, either. They're not all right. If you're hiding the relationship from your spouse or your boyfriend or your partner or if you're tamping down the significance of it, there is a reason.

These stories are everywhere. Adultery is common, very common. I share the territory with millions now and millions who went before and whole continents of people for which the practice is not as destructive as it is in the United States. Ezra Pound has been there, and Bob Marley. Henry the VIII, King David, Albert Einstein. Catherine the Great, François Mitterrand, Guinevere and Lancelot and all the denizens of Camelot (both of them), Prince Charles, Potiphar's wife, Mrs. Robinson, every pharaoh who ever lived, and a considerable number of popes, too (who were supposed to have been married to the church). We all have this in common, that we cannot resist the allure.

Its effects are everywhere apparent among strangers, too. If I see someone walking down the street, particularly if it's someone who looks unhappy or distracted, I always wonder if he has just found out. I wonder when was the last time that person got properly laid. I wonder when was the last time someone told her she was beautiful or thanked him for his love. I wonder if she left her home this morning smiling. I wonder if he argued the night before over the bills or the kids. I wonder if her birthday was celebrated or his last promotion was toasted or even if someone has recently made him carrot cake, which happens to be his favorite.

Is there not an occasion at least once a month to celebrate your mate? I know this sounds like so much treacle. But everyone walks around looking half-deprived. Of course they look that way through the filter of my own skewed marital perspective. Still, I would bet I'm not wrong. Many people don't do marriage well over the long run.

Which is kind of ridiculous. We are completely capable of loving people throughout the decades. Along with our children there are friends, for instance. Those are the most successful relationships of my life—more solid than the relationships with my siblings, with my parents, with my own spouse, with everyone except my sons. Bill once said to me, "If only you had treated me as well as you treated Jean, we might still be together." I have my doubts about this as an excuse. It is far too easy an explanation for how disastrously he went off the rails. But there is a point to be made.

It doesn't just have to be human relationships, either. Think of how people feel about their pets. Or about wine or knitting or shooting at quail flaring out of the brush. Think of the passion sports fans commit to their teams. Think of the power that generates. If the wattage of one football game's worth of devotion could be harnessed and used elsewhere—like in the marital bed or on a Saturday evening at a restaurant with your spouse—well, every union would be sparkling from base to crown like a Christmas tree.

I have never cataloged what I would want in a marriage. I might as well do it now. Since I can't have it, I will be profligate in the wanting. It's still a clean list. I want an arrangement in which love and passion mingle and last. I want a rock to lean against. I want sex to pierce reality and come blazing out the other side. I want to feel that someone has my back. I want it to be us against the world. I want marriage to be cool. I want the words *wife* and *husband* to resonate with joy. I want our intimacy to be inviolate. I want it all under one roof. I want the institution to deserve my energy and my commitment and the last decades of my life. I want what poet Jane

Cooper called "A radiance of attention / Like the candle's flame when we eat." I want to wake up next to a person who feels what I feel—that there is a constant, self-renewing joy in being with the other.

And of course I want allure to have less allure because the couple is weatherproof.

One day shortly after finding out about Bill, I told my brother that what I wanted almost more than anything was a normal, solid marriage. He said, "There is no such thing as a normal, solid marriage." I think he may have been right.

Not that it had approached normality, but after the emergency room debacle in October 2005, Bill and I were not to have a normal marriage ever again. We were not to have a marriage ever again. Bill moved out and into his rented apartment at a condo community a few miles away. It was a classic separated-spouse complex. I remember driving over once—and passing Susan on her way there—and seeing lots of empty take-out pizza boxes and one-liter soda bottles around the trash bins. Bachelor food. Food for those too desultory to cook.

In truth, I do not know how long Bill lived there. The boys did not go over often. Instead we created a template out of what seemed best for them from the examples of others. After New Year's Eve 2006, Bill came to our home, which became my home, and stayed there with the boys twice a week. I left. I went elsewhere, about which more later.

But in those early days, it was enough that my sons were in their own home with at least one parent. You try to come up with something that will shield the worst of it from your children. You will fail, of course, but there is some point to the trying. The way I saw our early arrangement, they could still sleep in their own beds.

They didn't have to pack off to some unfamiliar home. They could adjust slowly and over the months to the new rhythm of their lives. Eventually almost anything becomes a habit. And habit is welcome at such a needy time.

I realize I have to talk about my sons. That is a huge piece missing from this tale. But I do not want to drag them in any more than I have to. I do not want to say much because almost anything will sound self-serving and hollow, being only one deeply subjective view of their pain, and invasive, too.

Of their mind-set toward all of this, there are finally only a few words to say. Their childhood will reconcile itself in the future into two solid, secure young men, or it will not. That remains to be seen. I can only move forward with love and gratitude for what I hope is their resilience. What I wish is that the blessings of some stability they have had over the past half dozen years have been enough. And that the instability goes into the column of life experience, a kind of skill set that will be burnished over the decades and drawn on during a dim hour. I mostly had a stable, happy childhood and it ill-prepared me for what was to come. Perhaps the reverse will be true for my sweet sons.

What I do know, what any divorced parent knows, is that every difficulty my sons have going forward—trouble in school, problems with friends or relationships, loss or loneliness or lack of esteem—will trace in my mind back to these years and the mistakes we made and the ultimate mess their father made of our family. People console themselves with the idea that a one-parent home with less turmoil is superior to a combative home with both parents. I do not believe it. Children want their parents together. My own have said this. They want one family under one roof. It is not always possible to do this, but it is possible to know it. From that point of honesty, you have at least a chance of mitigating against it.

We kept busy that fall after Bill moved out. We went down to South Carolina. We maintained their former track of activity and sports and holiday celebrations. I had their friends over constantly. We bought geckos and rescued dogs and hauled home fish—anything to round out the loss in our home. We did not send out Christmas cards. It was too early to take a photograph that would do little more than underscore the absence. I do remember, though, that that first Christmas without Bill had more presents under the tree than any before it. We succumbed to the smother-gloom-with-gifts practice. It gave the appearance of solace, if not solace itself. This is truer when you're a nine-year-old.

For the better part of that fall, I felt barely alive. I remember getting out of my car in Princeton one October morning to do a newspaper story. I had an interview at an elementary school. I was meeting with a principal I had known for years and was relieved with the familiarity. But I was also keening with associations. I compared everything backward and, those days, nothing in the present seemed better. I saw this principal and I thought, The first time I met him I was married to Bill. The last time I saw him I was married to Bill. The last time I came to this school I was married to Bill. The last time I was in this parking lot. The last time I stood near this tree. The last time. The last time. As if this unrelenting mantra could link me back to those earlier years. As if the simple repetition would spin a wormhole out of the blackness in my head and transport the four of us back there. All I wanted to do was go back there.

I did this often. I tortured every hour with connections back to my former life. It must have been a form of recovery. If I go back over haunted ground often enough, it loses the heartbreak of association. But the healing was slow and laborious because I had a lot of ground to cover. I had to lay down new associations over the whole of my life. I had lived in Brandywine for eighteen years with Bill. Ghosts poured from every corner. I waited all day to go back to bed so I could fall asleep and forget. I came to think of the dark as almost holy.

During the day, I spent a lot of time examining the differences between having an affair and having one foisted on me. If one was better than the other. In the end, this was not true for me. The conduct of an affair was only marginally less miserable. I have spoken about the duplicity and the effect this has on your happiness. I was enthralled with the men I had affairs with, but I was never really happy. I do not know that deceit and happiness can coexist. And it is awful to long to be somewhere else, with someone else, to be divided against your own irreconcilable choices.

That fall, I also discovered a state of mind that my practice of adultery hadn't revealed. I discovered the narrow but pronounced luxury of being a chump. There is some liberation in it. When you are cheating, you are responsible for every moment of the deceit. Every lie falls heavily on your soul, and you carry it like a block of granite. It wears you out. When you have been mightily played, however, you have nothing to do but respond. You are pure reaction. You are light as air. You don't have to decide anything, as it has all been decided for you.

The spouse who leaves, the one who blows the doors off the marriage, never seems to fare as well in the end as the person who has been left. The latter has been emptied out and now the task is to slowly refill yourself. It is painful work, but it is also simple work.

There is only one direction out of your misery. Forward, however you conceive of it. I do not know that the cheater has this luxury. The betrayer's direction is more crooked, a drunken path between self-accusation and vindication. Of the several close friends I have whose marriages have ended in divorce, it is always the spouse who was left behind who recovers first and most.

Knowing how irresistibly I had been pulled toward adultery by any number of forces, I also thought long and hard about whether I was born a cheater and it was just a matter of time before my embarkation at that locale. If I had this possibility covertly tucked into some corner of my behavior or if it just happened in the moment because I allowed it to. From that point on, it was always much easier to go back to that place of betrayal, and back and back, because I'd already been there. I knew the terrain and I knew the way. I certainly didn't grow up assuming this about myself. But once the chance for departure was in front of me, I must say, I did not hesitate.

When I was younger, I surveyed the field and I wanted one, like Plato's perfect form. When I was married, I surveyed the field and had one, so I wanted many, like reality as Plato came to conceptualize it. Whether I changed or I simply grew into myself is one of those core mysteries that will never have a definitive answer. But I have my suspicions. If we use adultery to get out of a marriage, if adultery actually enriches a marriage, if it is absolutely blameless in the failure of a marriage that was bad in the first place—all of these are possible, too. They are not a part of my story. But most assuredly they are part of someone's.

There is also, finally, the question of forgiveness. As someone who has stormed the sanctuary of home and marriage often and with impunity, I think of forgiveness as a fair trade. In return for the betrayal I coiled around your neck, I will give you the forgiveness you deserve when you betray me.

In Bill's case, I don't know if it really was forgiveness that he gave me or if it was just resignation. He does have that history. He waits. Something carried him forward in our marriage. Maybe it was a kind of inertia, but it seemed like forgiveness. That is what I will go with in my final summation, in the way I behold our marriage.

For my own part, I forgave Bill his affairs nearly as soon as I found them out. Every time I found them out. This doesn't mean that the anguish goes immediately away. Far from it. Maybe even the reverse of it. It is harder to be sorrowful than it is to be hateful, particularly because I did not want our marriage to end. Nevertheless, since I had cheated also, I found it easier to forgive him his cheating. I understand allure. I understand how quickly it takes over. I understand the benign neglect that rumbles through a marriage. I understand falling into bed with someone just because it is so damned fun. Just because you want to.

Forgiveness exists for me in a separate room under lock and key. I keep it apart from the mess and the scorn and the bitterness that I still sometimes feel so that it remains untarnished and can be given that way. It stands apart. It is compartmentalized. It is the parterre I may well have tended above all the others.

At the same time, I must admit that I do not look for forgiveness from Bill. I think he has sailed beyond the right to offer that to me as a fair trade for what he has put us through since. The ten-year affair, the baby, the departure and nasty divorce, the marital finances wasted on them, the financial ruin that was handed my sons and me. There is a point of no return for people, and for comparisons, too. I would prefer to monitor my own absolution for the things I have done to him. But that is also a crooked path, glancing off guilt and coming to rest in a state of semipermanent homesickness. Not for exotica like Vanuatu. But for the larger meaning of home. By this point in my life, and now that I've lost it, that place has attained an exotica of its own.

STANDARD CANDLES

STANDARD CANDLE IS an astronomer's tool. It signifies
reliable luminescence, a pinprick of light in the weird
fabric of the universe whose strength of shine—its mag-
nitude—is measured and known among scientists. Standard candles are useful because if you have a quasar on this side of
the heavens and a quasar on that side, you can calculate the space
between them. You can use a mathematical equation based on their
shared luminosity. Standard candles help determine distance. They
help us get a grip on infinite complexity.

They make things seem not so unassailably vast.

In the fall of 2005 when Bill had finally walked out, I did not
know how to conduct the recovery. I did not know how to get my
hands around the loss so that my family could move forward. It was
paralyzing and very lonely since everyone had an opinion and no
one had an answer. Least of all me.

We used to have a backyard of acres where I could sprawl on
the lawn at night with my sons, with my dogs, with my neighbor
Katherine and her daughters, who often came over for marshmallows at the fire pit after Bill had absented himself. I made a habit of
scanning the night sky regularly to see if anything had changed.
Not in the sky, where everything mercifully remains the same in
our time, but in me.

I would look for signs of progress. I would start with the prover-
bial insignificance we all feel looking at the night sky and rejoice in
it, frankly. It helped to know that my anguish over my failed marriage and our uncertain future would cease utterly to matter in sixty
years. At that point I would be long gone and my sons, God willing,
would be old men. The sadness of this period would have resolved
itself in the revelation of their own lives. I liked the finality of that.
I took comfort in the magnificence of the night sky, my children
itching in the grass near me, and the knowledge that none of our suffering would leave a mark. And when Katherine was there, of course,
there were neighbors and burnt marshmallows for comfort.

I read books on astronomy to answer my new obsession. H. A.
Rey's book *The Stars* (oddly, the author of the *Curious George* series),
Timothy Ferris's *Coming of Age in the Milky Way*, and Carl Sagan's
Pale Blue Dot. And somewhere in those lost months someone put a
copy of Bill Bryson's *A Short History of Nearly Everything* into my
hands. I read it in four days. During that mad, hilarious dash through
Bryson's distillation of science and history, I came across these sentences: "Leavitt's genius was to realize that by comparing the relative
magnitudes of Cepheids at different points in the sky you could work
out where they were in relation to each other. They could be used as
'standard candles'—a term she coined and still in universal use."

I loved the poetry of the phrase. I loved the balance of the four
hard syllables that put me in mind of something rocking back and
forth, back and forth. Standard candle. Standard candle. I loved that
the scientific concept deepened from something seemingly familiar—
like wax candles at the dinner table—to something really out there,
and how I tripped over the difference between them and came up
smiling.

The idea of a standard candle resonated for me because it encompassed in a single phrase all the things I needed then: solace, a way through, the certainty that pain wouldn't last, a diversion bigger than my life, and a splinter of new intellectual knowledge about the universe that made it just that much more graspable. And it had nothing whatever to do with Bill and me.

I needed a new tool to navigate with. I found it in the concept of standard candles, a few lights blazing in the firmament to plow my way toward. "Standard candle" became more than a metaphor. It became something to fix my frayed focus on. I would steer as if moving from point of light to point of light, whatever those lights would reveal themselves to be. There were many, and I needed many. No one source of aid is going to help completely. You want to open your arms and say, Throw at us all the help you've got. Anything and everything is welcome.

Fortune-tellers, prayer beads, Ouija boards, tarot cards, palm reading, tea leaves, Zoltar, old women wearing head scarves: I would have used any of these if I thought they had something to offer. If you go to a fortune-teller, you have to condense most of what you want to know into one or two fundamental issues or you'll be there all day. Anyway, there should always be a few large questions in your head so you have something to think about while you're getting your car simonized. In my case, the questions that October came down to just one. I wanted to know if we would be all right.

A reporter friend of mine came into town to visit the boys and me that fall. Aware of the state of mental disrepair I had fallen into, he gave me one clarion bit of counsel. Quoting I have no idea who, he said, "When you're thirsty, drink. When you're tired, sleep."

I loved this. It was permission to do only what was necessary. Permission to love my children, take care of their needs, and then curl into an emotional hibernation. Grief saps your energy. The less you have to do, the better you can do it. So I zeroed down. Beyond taking care of the boys, I did almost nothing. It was the one time in my life when I existed simply and on an hourly basis.

Details became very important. If the general outlook was too overwhelming, I would focus on small things to pull me out of that drift. To bring me back to the moment at hand, where life was much clearer. If you pay attention to the curl of your son's hair, the teapot, the softness of the dog's ears, or the words on a printed page, then the nastier horizon recedes. Not entirely, but enough. This is the secret of Buddhism. And of getting by when you are miserable. Focus. Mindfulness. Awareness. Even the DNA-like twist of carpet nylons you are standing on is worthy of your attention as a means of diversion. I know this. I spent a lot of time down there. I am now well versed in carpet anatomy.

Work helped, too. I had gotten a freelance reporting job at a newspaper in Trenton, New Jersey, and was doing features and spot news again. I didn't feel like working. I didn't want to get out of bed. This is a familiar reaction among the divorcing legions. But work was a huge palliative. An awareness of how much larger the world is—that is comfort. Let me have an afternoon interviewing a professor of astrophysics to blow the weight off the whole day. You cannot talk about the Sloan Digital Sky Survey or dark matter or standard candles, for that matter, and still walk around lopsided with grief. I responded to the stimulation of work. The endless chattering in the back of my mind was held back, as by a breakwater. Whether or not we would be all right became less an urgent question than a philosophical one. Which made it easier to see the answer, to see that "Yes" answered back from a huge distance. It was an almost celestial, light-years, Oort cloud kind of distance. But it did answer back.

During that time, Bill and I talked on the phone several times a day, which, sweetly, was our pre-discovery level of conversation. That habit reasserted itself. I did not imagine that he was coming home. But we each needed the support of the other in some strange, antibiotic kind of way. Talking to a spouse is so very daily that it becomes an almost biological reflex. Sleep. Eat. Make egg salad. Talk to spouse. The sudden stoppage would have been like pulmonary distress.

I remember one phone call between us that lasted more than an hour, the boys given free rein with the television set downstairs while I was upstairs on the phone with Bill. It was nighttime and I kept the lights off in my bedroom, where I paced as we talked. The rug was striated with moonlight, and I kept walking through it and watching the pattern shift as I listened to Bill. He sounded frantic, wrestling with himself over his longing to return home and his decision to leave. He was very conflicted about his choice. Which family should he be with. Which choice would cause less pain. Which woman. Which child. What would work best for them. For him.

There is no way it could be otherwise. The separation of spouses, regardless of the circumstances, is like bones pulling apart. You have to rip away the sinew and the muscle and the dermis that your union has knit together over the years in order to be free of each other. Homeostasis is obliterated. It is actual pain.

We each said how much we missed the other. We remembered back to some halcyon past that in all likelihood didn't exist. But that night we shaped it with ease as we scrolled through memory after memory. We talked about the nights he used to walk through a dark campus to get to my college room. We talked about the trip to Montserrat with Robert and his first wife and the volcano that blew shortly after we left the island. We talked about the day he proposed to me. We talked about our shared friends—the priest, and J. D., and Bill's brilliant, sarcastic brothers. We talked about our difficult second birth and how scared Bill had been that he would lose us both. We talked about our old dog, Rogue, who bit at least three different people (two of whom deserved it). We talked about our first apartment in North Brunswick and how proud we had been of it, that space of ours that we paid for, that we filled with things that belonged to us as a real couple.

One memory led to another. It was mnemonic. Associative. And every sentence started with, "Do you remember the time . . ." It was a heartrending phone call. We have never had its like since. Maybe we could only have had it after Bill left, once the dice were thrown. We were free then of the burden of persuasion. I think we were trying to cast into form something we knew we were losing, to freeze our coupled life into a lasting object.

I know people will disagree. But there really is only one marriage.

It was such a good conversation that in some of those moments anything seemed possible. But I knew as I sliced back and forth through the pattern of moonlight that we would never get back together. Our history was cratered with spent artillery. We would not recover from this, and anyway, I did not understand how we would have a family with all the new pieces we had to work with. We were able to remember many moments of joy, but they couldn't be strewn over the wreckage enough to cover it all.

The way I look at it now, things happened in Bill's life that he was unequal to. He didn't handle the mess he created well at all, or he handled it by sidestepping it. He called forth a windstorm and then just waited in a defensive crouch to see how everything blew out and to see how everyone would react—me, the boys, our friends, my family, his family. I think he just laid down the whole situation and said, You all figure it out. It has become the pattern of our interaction nearly every day since. I have no real answers to anything from Bill.

It was the same way years ago when Bill found out about my own affairs. I cannot say we actually did anything to fix the situation apart from seeing a marital therapist. I recall us as simply staying together and moving on to the next milestone. A lurching, pathless trek away from the discovery of my adultery. We never sat down and declared definitively that we were going to stay together. We never discussed a breakup. I know that Bill was made miserable by my affairs. I also know that he tried simply by remaining in the marriage. In this way his inaction served me, served us. It jibed with my method of stitching the wound closed, which was simply to go forward determinedly. It worked for some things. We stayed together long enough to bring two beautiful sons into the world.

These were my means of recovery in the fall of 2005. At least in the beginning of that recovery. Habit, shortsightedness, focus, sons, work. Standard candles, all of them.

At the end of that year, I found a different sort of restorative. I had been sung the old saw, sort of as a joke, that if I needed to get over someone, I needed to get under someone else. This from another woman. I had never heard that phrase before. I have heard it a lot since. In reality, it is exactly what I did.

That U2 concert with Zane. Zane my friend. Zane from the "How do I do this?" phone call. Zane from Zane and Robert. Zane who was already divorced. Zane from high school. Zane whom I had actually dated when I was sixteen. I shot the only hole in one of my life at a local chip 'n putt golf course with him and Robert and Sherry. No one remembers this but me. I swear it happened. Way back then, Zane and I dated for about two months. There are photographs of us dressed up for our tenth-grade dance. Zane wore a blue corduroy three-piece suit of which he was enamored, and I wore really bad hair. He pounced on me in the car on the way home with his parents driving in the front seat. Many years later, I asked him what he imagined would happen then and what he was thinking. He answered that he was a teenage boy. He wasn't thinking.

Some twenty-five years after that backseat incident, in the fall of 2005, Zane called me to see if I wanted to go to the U2 concert with him. I think it was a mercy date. I think people were whispering behind my back. I had run into his mother and sister at a local farmer's market and they called Zane to say how gaunt I looked and how pale. Zane phoned that night and said, Come to the concert; it's in New York City. I was living by the hour then. I couldn't enter into a discussion about what that meant, so I told myself it didn't mean anything. Zane was an old friend. He had two tickets. I said yes and scribbled the date down. It seemed worlds away.

But as the night got closer, it started to feel like that one thing you are going to do in the month that everything else revolves around, the way the elderly have a doctor's appointment three weeks from now and can't do anything in the meantime because of it. That is what I had become. No, I can't go out for a drink with the Hens because I have the U2 concert. No, I can't go to the movies with my

sister because I have the U2 concert. I wanted to husband my re-
sources, as if this were going to be the only thing that would ever
happen to me again and so I should ration all other distractions.
Spread them out over the long years ahead. Oh yes. You can become
quite maudlin. Cue the violin.

On the night of the U2 concert, the boys went to stay at my
parents' house, where my mother would make them "monkey meat"
(creamed hamburger in disguise) and let them fall asleep on the
bedroom floor with the television on. Scandalous. I drove to New
York City. On the way up I must have talked with three friends on
the phone, each of them hearing the same version of how exhausted
I was, how sick I was of being unhappy. I'm sure they were sick of
hearing it. It had been eleven months of hell. I felt absolutely
weighted, as if someone had tied a truck to each ankle and then
thrown the gears into reverse.

As I see it now, that was another standard candle. When you
start to get bored with your own misery you are on the first rung of
recovery and you are beginning to climb back up. You add one thing
at a time back into your life just as a break from monotony. Instead
of feeling wretched, I will start reading again. Instead of feeling
wretched, I will start working out again. I will start answering the
phone. I will consider the city. I will think about coffee with friends.
You start putting in the pieces until eventually what you have is an
actual life. It resembles what you had before, but it won't be exactly
the same. It will be recognizable, but off-kilter. For the first time in
nearly a year, I felt a faint rumble of curiosity about what it would
look like.

What did it look like that night? It looked like there was a lot of
traffic leading up to the Lincoln Tunnel. It looked like everyone in

217

New Jersey was going through it. It looked like Times Square had been taken over by insurgents. I don't like driving in the city. I'm used to driving with cows on one side of the road. In my hometown I navigate by red barns and empty fields and that place where I hit the deer once. I started to panic just a little. I remember thinking, Maybe I should just get out of here.

At that moment my cell phone rang. It was Zane. He was calling to see how far away I was. When I answered he heard the break of nervousness in my voice. "There's a lot of traffic here," I told him, as if it were not apparent to him. He had already parked at the hotel where I had booked a room. He talked me through the labyrinth, speaking into the cell phone reassuringly right up to the moment I pulled into the valet area and stopped next to him. I got out and hugged him. He wore a red jacket and smelled like fresh laundry. And his hair was shorter. I hadn't seen him but once in five years.

It was a great concert. Patti Smith opened. Then U2 played. Then Patti and Bono sang a Beatles cover song. I'm not sure it could have been better. Even our seatmates were great. And the walk through the freezing streets afterward was great. We had a great talk at a café with great vodka and pasta. A great waiter. Great taxis outside. Great hats on people's heads. Great asphalt on the sidewalks and great trash in the gutters. I was out with another man and it was all right. In fact, it was great. Everything was great. I felt human.

Back at the hotel room, which we had agreed to share, I was twitching again with curiosity. What was going to happen here? I had adored Zane for years, but only as my friend. That he happened to be very good-looking was still beside the point. Yet I was just on the edge of realizing something. The horizon had begun cranking open.

I had booked a hotel room imagining—and while no one be-lieves me, it is the truth—that at the most we'd have a night of sweet affection. That would have been enough. I was so starved of it that I would have been happy just hearing Zane move about the room. Earlier that fall a friend of mine, a man with whom I was cycling, put his hand on the back of my bare neck. I nearly swooned at his touch. I had missed the press of human flesh. I hadn't had sex in months and months. Even before he moved out, Bill had been ob-serving some sort of perverse misplaced loyalty to Susan by keeping me at bay. That night with Zane, all memory of the past year was vaporized.

Zane was in his double bed across the room. I was in mine. We had both just sort of climbed into our own spaces. Well. Maybe that was how it would end. He seemed firmly entrenched and quite comfortable over there on his side of the room. I couldn't under-stand how anyone could be so calm under the circumstances. I'm not that calm even when I'm asleep. If nothing were to happen, we were still a man and a woman with a history of friendship, alone in a hotel room, and both of us single. Calm was not a factor. I began to want something else. Zane? Zane.

Maybe I should just say something to, you know, test the situa-tion. Poke a stick into the closet. "I know this sounds like bullshit," I said aloud to the dark, "but I really am cold." I really was cold. And then within about two seconds, Zane was there, next to me. And I wasn't cold.

Few people can write about sex without ruining it. I can only put down the way Zane made me feel and the small details of that night—the sweat on his back, the beads from his leather necklace swaying over me, the strength in his arms, the sound of his breath breaking, his face looking down at mine. We were awake all night. He was so beautiful. I was almost weak with joy. And the mystery of this man, whom I had known since sophomore year in high school, was both answered and broadened. I had loved hanging out with him when I was a young woman. Now I stared as if at someone new. The very presence of a man in my life again was astonishing. The fact that it was Zane seemed unreal but sweetly obvious, as if I were tumbling into a rabbit hole I myself had begun digging decades before.

Other than me, no one I knew was surprised at this. Least of all Zane.

The next morning, I called my mother from our hotel to tell her that I might be home an hour or two later than expected, that I was still with Zane. Up to that point in my life, my mother had seemed the most puritanical of women. Straitlaced, firmly grounded in strict propriety, modest, careful. I had never heard her yell. I had never seen her tipsy. I had never even heard her curse. How I sprang from her loins is a mystery to me. But she was to astonish me that day, too. She said, Stay Wendy. Stay as long as you want. I am the happiest mother in the world right now because you suddenly sound like my daughter again.

Several weeks later, a kind of waterloo. I did not mean for Zane to become a symbol of comeuppance. He was more important to my life than that. And I am not big on the concept of revenge. It muddies your soul. And yet I can't deny the sweetness of that evening when Bill discovered that I was spending my time with someone else and who that someone else might be.

Bill and I had fallen into a pattern that fall so that he could visit the boys. Eventually he would come over for nights in a row to be with them, but at that early point he would visit for a few hours twice a week, from after school until bedtime. I would leave my home for those hours. Bill didn't know where I went, and he didn't ask. I'm sure if he thought about it at all, he thought I was out with the Hens.

On that particular December night, Zane and I were having a drink at the Temperance House, where one year before I had told two girlfriends about my resolution to be a really good wife in 2005. I had had no idea how good I would become, as a wife, as a woman trying to keep her family intact, and still manage to fail. Yet there I was with Zane at the threshold of something completely new.

Zane lived in northern New Jersey, so we had agreed to meet at the bar, arriving there in separate cars. Afterward, we were going back to my house. I asked Zane how he imagined we would accomplish that because Bill would be there waiting until I got home. If Zane wanted to wait at the bar until Bill left my house, that was fine. If he wanted to wait out in his car until Bill drove away, that was fine, too. Whatever made him comfortable. But Zane didn't want to do any of this. He told me, What you are doing is all right. It is okay to have another man in your life. He said he preferred to meet Bill face-to-face because then everything would be out in the open. I thought this quite noble.

Zane knew Bill, of course. Not well, but for many years. Zane and his ex-wife had been to our wedding; Bill and I had been to theirs. We had been out for dinner together once. Zane had come to a party at our home two years before. The boys knew him as one of the best friends of my youth. But Zane's appearance at my house by my side at that hour would leave no doubts about what I had been doing lately with my spare time. I had already told the boys that I was dating Zane. I had said nothing to Bill.

Zane drove back home with me after midnight in his own car. So that Bill saw two sets of headlights coming down the driveway, heard two sets of feet walking through the garage and up the stairs, heard the sound of me—his wife—talking. With another man. When Zane and I walked into the kitchen and Bill laid eyes on him, Bill blanched. Literally lost his color. I have never seen that happen so obviously. He stared at Zane as if he were a stranger, as if shock took the place of recognition. Which I suppose it did. Zane said simply, "Hi, Bill." I don't remember if Bill answered. I do remember that he very quickly left the house.

I have to say that in light of everything, it was a good moment. I felt, of all things, pride. Not an ego-driven, braggart's pride. Not a vengeful pride. Just simple pride at having found my own footing in spite of everything that had happened. When you are on the receiving end, infidelity makes you pathetic, almost contemptible in your victimhood. It is humiliating. It was good to be able to look Bill square in the eye again and feel an equal. I liked that I had found some measure of absolution despite him.

The next day he called and yelled at me for setting a poor example for our sons by bringing another man home. Considering his own history, I didn't figure I needed to answer that charge. I would work it out with my sons without his interference. As we had begun doing everything else.

For many months afterward, my family remained hanging in that purgatory. Our divorce was on the horizon, but neither Bill nor I dealt with it energetically. I just wanted us all to rest for a while. Let the ball settle. Live a routine that was more or less normal. Suddenly normal wasn't boring. Normal was bliss. Although he lived ninety minutes away and there were as yet no plans for him to move closer, Zane and I had a blossoming relationship. I was happier than I had been. I was a better mother because I wasn't sobbing into the couch anymore. The boys and I remained in our home alone with the dogs and the lizards and the occasional frog or captive bird. And on some of those weekends, Zane was there, too.

Some things remained the same. The morning jog to the school bus, the friends over after school to play, the dogs throwing up on the best rug in the house almost as if they aimed. Paintball became a huge fascination, and airsoft guns. There were boys and boys and boys at our home. In the fall of 2006, a hot-air balloon landed in our backyard. Bill happened to be there visiting, and after all the clients disembarked from the balloon basket the pilot handed him a bottle of champagne in thanks for the landing pad. I took it from Bill, shaking my head. No, I said. This is not your right anymore. You chose not to live here. I get the champagne. Small comfort. It was crappy champagne.

The stasis did not last. Well before the economy fell apart in late 2008, Bill lost his job when the company he worked for was reorganized. He did not look for another job then or since. It has been five years since he has worked. Whatever his reason, he threw up his hands and did nothing and spent our savings on child support— for all three of his children. Things spiraled down from there. Our savings disappeared. Our finances tanked. Acrimony took over and we stopped talking altogether. The boys and I were largely on our own, are largely on our own. It's an old story.

I remember the afternoon in January 2009 when I told my sons that we were going to have to sell our home and move elsewhere. There was no more money to sustain it. I could not support us in that house by myself. My oldest son was fourteen at the time, my youngest, ten. I chose a Friday afternoon for our talk so that they would have the weekend to let the news sink in and so I could have them close to me for the first few shell-shocked days, as if that would help. When things are going to be bad, you make a grab for even the smallest pieces of glitter.

I picked up the boys at school. I pulled down the driveway and put the car in park and said that I needed to tell them something. I was dying inside. It was worse than having to tell Bill about an affair. I just turned to look at them and said, We are going to have to sell the house and move. And then I waited. I couldn't launch into an explanation or a defense. There was no defense. And I wanted to see what they wanted to know first. It is the only way I have learned to deliver bad news.

The boys were stunned, but only momentarily. Then there were tears and fury. My oldest son screamed out of the car, going upstairs to his room, where he punched a hole through a window. My youngest wouldn't get out of the car but sat with big, silent tears rolling down his face. He was worried about the dogs, the trampoline, the woods, if we could still walk down the creek when it froze over. It was one of the worst moments of my life, particularly since the oldest tore away and the youngest stayed put. Whom do I follow or stay with? Who needs me more in the moment? And after all, what can I say that will be of any use to their pain?

Everything that had happened to them over the past few years—their father's other family, his departure, their half-brother enrolled at their elementary school such that they passed him in the hallways—they had accepted with more or less equanimity. Some of it was beyond their understanding. They were still very little when I first told them about Susan and their father's baby. It didn't seem to make much sense to them at the time and, frankly, it didn't seem to faze them much, either. Either they didn't get it or they didn't care to get it. When Bill moved out, one of my sons said, "It's not all that different. Dad was never around anyway." Which was sadly true.

But the sale of the house was something else entirely. We were going to have to move, to leave our home. The adults in their lives, their most trusted people, had let them down brutally.

At that point, I didn't know where we were going to live next. There was not enough money to buy a house and not a whole lot to rent one. I had to tell them about the move, though, because the realty company was hanging a sign in a week. Presumably, Realtors would start coming through just after that. There would be strangers in their home, appraising it with a cold, buyer's eye. Home should be inviolate. How you explain to a child that it isn't inviolate, that in fact few things in life actually are . . . well, all the things I had learned over the past few years were useless to that task.

There had been ground gained since the end of 2005 in resting, in reestablishing a small kind of normalcy for my boys and myself. It had been a good time in our lives, and I'm grateful for it. But as I see it now, it may just have been a way station. It was a temporary post so we could catch our breath before we bridged the next distance using any point of light, standard candle or otherwise.

WRECKAGE

IN THE SPRING of 2010, I got a phone call from my Realtor. People were on their way over to look at our house on Brighton Road, which had recently gone on the market. I had to get out of there before they arrived. But I remember pausing to fix a pillow on the couch and put a glass away in the cabinet. I didn't do this for them. I did it for me, because that's how I left my home when I went out. Ordered. What I wanted to do for them was scribble a note on the counter so that they would see it. I wanted to tell them, "We live here. Now. You might at some point but not until we go. Please be human about this."

Like everywhere else that year, our township in Pennsylvania was in a major housing market slump. Still, I respectfully refused the advice of my Realtor to clear the photographs and news clippings off my refrigerator. They plainly identified me as a liberal, a marcher for causes, a traveler, a mother with two sons who play football and roll in the mud and lie in the grass with their dogs. All of these could argue against me in some future sale, I was told.

There were taped photographs of me holding a bottle of vodka standing next to my brother. And hiking on vacation in Saint Lucia with Zane, who had become a part of our lives. There was a photo of my older son with a yellow bucket on his head and of my younger running tan and shirtless down the driveway. There was even one of Bill way down in the corner, holding our oldest son as a baby.

I never emptied the mantelpiece, as I was advised to, of its clutter: a black-and-white photograph of my mother on her wedding day; a boomerang I got in Australia; a hurricane lamp; a blow-dart gun and pouch of blow darts sent to my sons from my friend in Chile. I remember my surprise and puzzled delight at their receipt of that oddball gift. Considering Wayne Honey, the two-tour Vietnam War vet and postal worker who sent it, it's reserved in the extreme. Wayne once sent them the dried-out carcass of an alligator he had killed by himself in Brazil.

In our living room were displayed rather proudly—as if I had something to do with their origins—all my copies of Dostoyevsky's novels, of Maxine Kumin's poetry, of children's stories I had read to my sons in the chair nearby still covered with dog hair. I did not vacuum up the fur even though it might have gotten all over the Realtor and his clients. I left over the fireplace the illustration of Tolstoy that Zane had drawn and given to me for our first Christmas together. And the peacock feathers that a friend had brought from a sculpture park, and the blown-glass bottle plucked from the bottom of a harbor in St. Thomas.

My Realtor was worried these artifacts would cloud a buyer's decision. He told me that buyers needed to see themselves in a home unmolested by someone else's Stuff. But I was less concerned about the buyers. I was stubborn about our placeholders staying where they were. Not because I resented the coming of those droves, but because I viewed them as anthropologists on a field trip, and so why would they care? They arrived at our home with the dispassionate gaze of the scientist. Their mission might result in an offer if the things they saw pleased them, but not right away. We still lived there. The human lives framed by those walls and the pieces of us on display spoke volumes. I wanted buyers to notice because that seemed appropriate to their privilege and to our coming loss.

I am not talking here about the loss of people. I am talking about the loss of things. About physical wreckage. Apart from the psychic wreckage, the house represents the biggest collateral damage in a divorce. You cannot just walk away from your home, even though at every point along the way you will want to. You will want to avert your eyes. The day the FOR SALE sign went up on our front lawn, I sat in the car and sobbed until my shoulders hurt, and then after took my sons to the toy store for no particular reason at all.

The dispersal of Stuff when a home is splitting apart casts the whole concept of divorce into hard form. Up to a point, you have merely talked about it. You have told your children. You have made the decision that you are breaking up or had it foisted on you after months and stupid months of energy wasted. But you still go to your own bed at night and come awake at three A.M. and trip toward your accustomed bathroom. You get up and feed the dog out of the same bowl under the same window, and your children catch the bus out in front of their home as usual.

The reality of an ending, though looming, doesn't compute yet. How could it? Everything is still in its place. Your mind surveys the environment and argues against that reality by reacting so reassuringly to all the Stuff, as if its very heft and placement will anchor you there forever.

And it will, until you start taping bubble wrap around the troll sculptures that one son shaped in kindergarten. Or choosing between the "My Dog Beefy" report that the other wrote in fifth grade and the "Book of Weather Poems" he composed in sixth. Then it becomes real. You have to pack some of that stuff up. You have to throw some of it out. You have to watch it all march past you on the way through the door, and the groove it wears feels as though it's cutting into your skin.

There is a reproach in items. Not to anthropomorphize too dramatically, but there were pieces of furniture that actually scowled in my direction as they were going out of the house. Tables that bumped doorjambs unnecessarily. Lamps that blew their bulbs. Mirrors that cracked although they had been taped to infinity for their own safety. And one old pine hutch—oh, that harpy, that eighteenth-century Irish sideboard—that refused to fit through the doorway without scraping the hell out of the paint. Failure, they all said before hitting the moving truck. Divorce. Ending. Loss.

When my grandfather died in 1982 mere months after my grandmother, their home had to be cleaned up and emptied. I was not a part of this, being off at college and swept up in the central affairs of my own life, dumb to all else around me in the way that only a twenty-year-old can be. But at Thanksgiving when I came home, I found myself confronting a huge storage trailer that contained their Stuff. Their books, which had spent all of my life arrayed in perfect order on bookshelves in their home, were crammed into boxes. Their shotguns and rifles were tucked into padded cases. Their chairs, their figurines, their framed photographs, were all shoved into corners not befitting the dignity of their worth. It was a moment of profound realization for me that this is what life comes to whether you are married, divorced, happy, poor, old, or single. All your Stuff at the end crammed into a few boxes.

This is not an argument for having fewer things so much as a caution against future irrelevancy. I understand why divorcing spouses fight to the death over objects. From birth we are associative creatures. People brag about the three-year-old who remembers that an aunt wore red on the last family occasion. The three-year-old remembers that the aunt wore red not because he's a budding genius, but because by nature we associate everything we see and do. We trace it all back to something remembered, and thus we learn.

It is a pattern that can become burdensome later in life. As when you have to get rid of your grandfather's books. Or pack up and dispense with your household because of divorce. Every item trails associations, and they are fiercest then, and they will bleed you dry. And so you fight your spouse for the paintings and the hutches and the toy boxes and the snow shovels. You want them and all the associations they carry not to vanish. But they will vanish.

We had bought the house off Brighton Road seven years before, in January 2003. I had a stomach virus that month at the same time as my youngest son, who was then about two years old. I took the victory phone call from my Realtor between turns throwing up in the bathroom—propping him against the wall, then leaning over him to lose it myself. I had trouble returning the glee in my Realtor's voice: "You've bought a house!" It did occur to me that the new home would have more space in the bathroom in case this scene ever played out again.

What troubles me now is the choice we made. Had I known about Susan, who by that point had moved into the area and was living only a mile away from us, I would not have moved out of our first home, the one we bought shortly after we were married. Small but full of character and covered in good Pennsylvania fieldstone, that home was perfect. We should have stayed. So much would have been different, including and especially the fact that I could have supported my sons there financially and we would not have had to move. Small meant cheap, and the mortgage was nearly paid off. The boys and I could have lived there forever with almost no struggle. And our neighbors were wonderful.

This was the sort of scene that played out nearly every day in that neighborhood: One afternoon I was coming home from my doctor's office, eight months pregnant with my second son. It was January and our walkway was glazed over, slick with ice. I took a couple of steps along it and then stopped, terrified that I would fall and harm my baby. I stood there for a moment, trying to puzzle out the next move, when from down the street I heard the shrill call of a neighbor's teenage son. "Mrs. Plump," Jonathon yelled, "do you need help?" And then he ran up the street and offered his awkward adolescent arm, steadying me into the house.

How could we have wanted to live anywhere else?

I think about these people even today, this refrain repeating in my mind: We should have stayed, we should have stayed. We did not. We thought we needed a bigger home, urged on by the exhortations of the American dream. I was following the blueprint left for me by generations. Bill, I can only imagine, was simply following.

The house off Brighton Road was a bargain for a home in that sheltered enclave in Brandywine. It had twelve acres. This was shocking in itself because some developer hadn't showed up at the front door before we bought it with a fistful of dollars and a plan to build sixteen homes within its borders. It had a small, shallow pool. Fields. Trees filled with hawks and owls (not simultaneously). And a creek that ran across the bottom of the property like a footer.

Someone told me the home made her wish her own sons were still young so that she could raise them there. That pretty much clinched it for me. Like her, I could see boys in that big yard. Boys and footballs and scratched knees and cases of poison ivy and small tents arrayed and nights of snowfall and full moons.

However, I suspected, then and to this day, that the house was haunted. Not by some violent bloody presence that flung knives at you and vivisected the pet bunny. Just some bitchy, lurking little ghost who liked to muck with people's lives. As soon as we had bought it, I was in doubt—why was this house so inexpensive compared with others around it? I wondered if there were a tribe of Lenni Lenape Indians buried under one of the fields or a seam of arsenic running through the ground beneath that leached into the groundwater and made your hair fall out. (I'm a chick—hair is important.) Otherwise I could not account for it.

Of course, later I did realize why. That house eats marriages. The two previous owners' unions had gone down in flames. The first couple lost the house to a sheriff's sale. The second couple had a drug problem. The wife was carted away in handcuffs one afternoon, and a divorce with sinister accusations followed. Both that husband and wife, incidentally, showed back up one afternoon in quite the state years later, long after we'd moved in. I found her hysterical at my front door, missing the house and her own associations there. Her ex-husband showed up hours later after she was gone, clucking over her hysteria and building his case in spite of my obvious disdain for him. Then later that night, she snuck into his condo and tried to stab him.

Really, it takes the onus off Bill and me. The mess of our marriage was not about us. It was about the house on Brighton Road. That place is nuts.

When we moved in I invited a beloved friend, a Sikh and a yogi, to come and blow some sage into the closets and around all the doors. Exorcise the demons. Soothe the household gods. Let them all know that we were there and we were going to make it right, have a beautiful marriage, raise our sons well, and then cuddle grandchildren on the back porch amid the wisteria.

Despite the sage, things did not go as planned. There were some early signs. Before we moved in, there were painters in the house, covering over the lurid shade of red on the walls the previous owners must have chosen after an evening of drinking Jell-O shots. One afternoon, one of the painters heard a loud crash in the kitchen and ran through it and outside onto the back porch to find a huge red-tailed hawk flopping on the deck in its death agony. It had flown straight into the big kitchen window and snapped its beak. That poor, magnificent bird died cradled in the painter's arms. We buried it in the field. I should have known right there.

Many years later, during the months our home was on the market, I tried to box things up secretly, plucking items from around the house but never all from one room, thinking this would prevent my sons from noticing. I wanted it to look right up to moving day as if we still lived there, forestalling the moment they would look at their home and say, Yes, now we understand about divorce.

So as people came through with my Realtor, they must have noticed that the Brighton Road house looked like a real home, with other people's stuff all over the place. They marched through, commenting on the outdated kitchen and the age of the house and its acreage and how wild it was—meaning they thought I had not kept it up and would detract from the asking price accordingly. Well, I hadn't kept it up. We were running out of money. We were nearly broke, the boys and I.

It wouldn't be an easy sell. Prospective buyers could see quite clearly that my older son's room was a mess. He was a young teenager, after all, and that is what they do. I had been asked to make more of an effort to keep it spotless. But had I cleaned it too much, it would belong more to them than to him. He still inhabited that room in every way, and I needed to honor that. My younger son's room was spare, almost monastic, and that said something about him, too. Because that was how he wanted it. Although I had been asked to spruce it up—"Get some color in the room; paint a balloon on the wall"—I did not embellish. It was his space.

And my room—immaculate, white, clean. It was an attempt to make order out of the ruin of my family. I thought it would communicate its own message. We are not a disaster—see how white my room is.

What all these people probably did not sense by looking around our dining room filled with Tuscan vases (we traveled there in 2003 when we were still a family) or our den with its twisted branches of driftwood hung on the wall (plucked from a beach in South Carolina we no longer visited) was that there wasn't a husband or a father living there anymore.

The morning in October 2005 when Bill moved out for good, I had stolen a sneaker out of his luggage in an effort to keep some small, stupid part of him. I can picture myself rummaging through his suitcase. While he was outside packing up his car, I was frantically grabbing at some artifact that would stand in for him over the long months of recovery. I could have taken a cotton shirt that carried his cologne or his toothbrush or the book he was reading. That would have made more sense. But I was not operating with a full deck. My husband was leaving. Our family was divided. Wreckage was everywhere. I became obsessed with the possibility that an object could convey the person. This was the irrational logic of a child or of an adult under siege.

I thought if I could hold on to that sneaker, as silly as it sounds now, it would mean something. It would mean, possibly, a return to the family. Bill would have to come back and get it. I found portent and meaning in this. It would be one of the habits I would have to unlearn in the coming months—not to read into every development. Not to analyze. Not to take the owl we found perched on a back porch chair one morning as an omen. Not to read into the new litter of groundhogs or the bark of a fox running along the creek at night. Sometimes a hawk winging across the backyard is just a hawk winging across the backyard.

I chose the sneaker from all the other possible objects in that bag. I had hauled it out and stuffed it up under the green couch in the family room. But only one. The other sneaker I left in his bag so that he would ask himself, Where the hell is its mate? A leading question. That would serve as a connection back to me. I have it, I would be able to answer. I have your sneaker. I have your rakes and shovels. I have your home and your dog and your albums. I have your sons. I have the pieces of your life. They are still here. And if you come home, I will help you put them back together.

During the spring of 2010, when I was slowly cleaning out the house, I found that sneaker under the couch. It startled me with the rawness of its associations. I remembered well the anguish I had felt on stealing it out of Bill's bag. I no longer felt that way. I had come out the other side. I took that sneaker outside and tossed it into the Dumpster, watched it spiral through the backyard and fall in among all the broken oddments. I wasn't angry. I was intrigued with the person I had been that day. Oh, I was sad, and that sad artifact brought it all back. The pointless, desperate grab that you make to hold on to someone.

What a pathetic emblem the Dumpster became, too. Even the name sucks. Dumpster. Dump your whole life into it. Feel like you're down in the dumps. Dump everything. What a dump. Some days I couldn't bear to look in it and see the Day-Glo fur of stuffed animals my sons had slept next to poking up out of the refuse. The urgency of those items as they filled the Dumpster was annihilating. They said, If you are going to toss us out, then we are going to torture you before we go. We are going to remind you of babies and fish tanks and Christmases and the crooked, overly wrought lettering of kindergartners and the smell of tempera paint and school glue and paintball games and breast-feeding in the rocking chair and how young your sons used to be and how it was all brought to ruin.

Moving is one thing. Moving because your marriage is over and your family is smashed is another. It ought to be disallowed. That sort of avoidable pain should be a felony.

These were not details that would be readily obvious to my Realtor and his buyers, who could not help but walk coldly through our home. So I wanted to spell it out for them. I wanted to say: As in every other house for sale you visit, the families who have lived there have left a haunt of memories. I discovered them myself when we first moved into this house—the old marijuana joint in the closet (too old, as it turns out), the postcard from Majorca under the cabinet, the crocus bulbs a former owner planted that came up each spring like someone else's surprise. Now we had laid down our own dusting of memory over these.

Maybe buyers would notice it as they walked by a particular spot and shuddered through some vibration we'd left behind. There we watched a storm of lightning bugs rise from the field. There my older son fell off the porch railing and didn't breathe for thirty heart-crushing seconds. There the boys played on the tree swing while I read all the *Harry Potter* books to them. There my younger son found a salamander, tadpoles, crayfish. There I stood outside in the snow and bayed like an animal the night I found out my husband had a baby with someone else. There I hid his sneaker. There, after Bill moved out, I made love with another man, in awe that this could happen for me again. There he chased me amorously up the back porch steps with his boots untied. There he parked his truck and walked down to meet me in the field, a smile lighting his handsome face.

The associations keened, but the buyers were oblivious. They saw instead a house where carpets would need to be reinstalled and the kitchen cabinets replaced and the dog door in the basement closed up. Once I found a set of buyers still in the kitchen when they were supposed to be finished and out of there. They were casually surrounded by architects and paint swatches, laughing around my table. I seethed at them. I threw them out only minutes before the boys got off the school bus and made their little way down the drive. I was very protective of those days as they were dwindling down. It was a single-cell existence of tending my boys and getting through the packing up surreptitiously.

On such a canvas it was easier to see everything more clearly. So in the middle of feeling like hell, I was also aware of the beauty of our lives at that home, the holy loss of it. My youngest son waking up for school and climbing all warm and cottony into my lap. My oldest son playing with his friends out in the backyard so that their voices carried in through the open windows. My two sons sitting on top of their tree house, both reading, becalmed, for once not trying to push each other off.

I was not bitter about having to leave, mostly. I was sad. The boys were very sad. For some reason, I wanted buyers to know. It reminded me of the beginning of the housing crisis when a friend called to crow about a second home they'd bought down south for a bargain. A bargain. It's only a bargain to you, I thought. Buy it if you must, but for everyone's sake, think first. Pay the slightest homage to someone else's loss. It could be us or someone like us. It could be you.

In just seven years, for example, our own home was fully inhabited and it reflected all kinds of intense loves. Our misfortune was common enough, particularly that year when everyone was losing homes and being foreclosed on. But it brought buyers a measure of good luck. I wanted them to live there and enjoy our home—the library, the claw-foot tub, the hammock stretched between two spruce trees, the creek the deer thundered through each fall—but I wanted them to know how they came to be there and at what price.

Anyone can practice this courtesy. I do it this way even today. I drive past other homes and think about the people who live in them. Everyone seems to have one. They make it look so easy. How do they do it—and by this I mean simply, Do they *know* they are there? Do they use that awareness well? Do they acknowledge their luck? It is hell to lose your home. They should know this. They should be aware of their lights coming on at night and flooding the windows with warmth. Their cherry trees flowering. Their yards filling up with footballs, Frisbees, thrown newspapers. All the detritus of normal, domestic life that now makes it hard for me to breathe. Every bit of our home life had a limit impossible to ignore. February was my youngest son's last birthday in that home; my older son's was in May. We had a last Christmas, a last snowfall, a last flowering of dogwoods.

When I went to bed at night, long after the Realtor and his clients had left, my fingers would reach around the curve of the foyer wall in the dark until just . . . there, when I would feel the light switch for the upstairs hallway. I would flick it on and think how long it took me to figure out which light switch worked which light. And how precious was that simple knowledge of one house. It was another kind of intimacy.

People asked me where we would live next. At the time I had no idea. What I did know is where we had been. And what I cared about is that they knew, too. In this way, we all move forward in some manner of conjoined fate. Not completely abandoned to our own weird, solitary destinies, but part of a wheeling whole. When you acknowledge that, you give us and everybody else pawing through their own wreckage some reprieve in empathy, small but welcome. It is what we use to go forward in hope, pushing off from one home and touching down at another.

Infidelity has laid down its footprint on the calendar of my year. Now along with tracking my sons' birthdays and the birthdays of friends and holidays and quarterly tax deadlines, I also track the anniversary of finding out, the anniversary of Bill leaving, the night of my first date with Zane, the day in August when the moving vans came and loaded everything up with devastating efficiency, as if there were no need for grief.

The boys and I live now in a small rented home, bang up against a noisy road. It's so small, in fact, that I can vacuum the entire house from one outlet in the den. It is very old. People have died in its bedrooms, which likely means it has ghosts, too. I had a serious talk with the staircase when we moved in, just to be clear. We are a family in need of sanctuary, I told it. We are tired and we have been through a lot and we need stability. We need the embrace of a reliable home. Please be kind. No more wreckage.

I did in fact later hear that the people who bought our home on Brighton Road—a multigeneration family who got the place for a dime but luckily did not know I'd already gotten two foreclosure notices—added a massive addition and changed it into a big old white elephant. They were later besieged with sudden basement flooding and water leaks and sinking backyards. There had been no such problems when we lived there. No mold. No watermarks. No floating basement toys. They were mystified.

I, however, was not. By then I had become pretty comfortable with the proximity of ghosts.

YES, I SAID

KEEP COMING BACK to two scenes that collapse the reality of Bill and me as a married couple into something clearer and discernible. They do not enclose the whole of our marriage, but as explicators of adultery they come close. From the perspective of many years later I look back on these scenes and cock my head like the family dog at their enduring intensity.

For me, it would be that bar in South Carolina where I was drinking in 1990 with Steven, the man who would become my lover later that night. Steven and I are sitting at a booth. We are surrounded by people we know. I had caught that shark earlier in the afternoon and my arms are wrung out from reeling it in. I am slightly drunk. Steven is laughing and his gaze is locked on me. I can feel his desire. There is a lot of noise and clamor, drunken fishermen and carousing tourists and half-drowned music in the background. And then Steven kisses me. In the middle of all that tumult, we are suddenly pressed together. There is no interruption to the scene apart from us kissing and no doubt one or two of those people around us thinking, Aren't they both married? And neither one of us caring a damn.

For Bill, it would have to be that July 2004 morning or night—I don't even know which—when he walked into a hospital delivery room to attend the birth of his son with another woman. The boys and I were away for a few weeks, packed off early by Bill's suggestion that we start our vacation without him and he would try to join us later if work let up. A neighbor later told me that our home one night in the middle of that month was flooded with lights. Every light in every window seemed to be on and the house was ablaze straight through the night, such that she had to close curtains to block it out. So that must have been the night.

I know what I was thinking at that bar in South Carolina. I was thinking, This is fantastic. I love this. I love the thrill of this stranger, this new man. I love all this noise around me receding because my ears are filled with the pressure of adrenaline now, the rush of desire. I love that I feel like this again. I have missed it. I was not thinking about marriage or about Bill. I didn't care. I know I didn't care. I can admit this now, over twenty years later. I wouldn't have admitted it then because I just did not want to.

And what was Bill thinking in that hospital? I have no idea. I still have no idea. One day when we are very old, I would like to sit down with him and ask. Maybe we will get to the point where the injuries done to each other don't matter and everything distills down to simple curiosity. What happened, Bill? What were you thinking that night and every night for the preceding nine months? The preceding ten years? What was your plan? How did you survive what must have been an agony of waiting? I wish I knew these things now. In all likelihood, I will never know them.

So marriage for us comes down to mystery. The mystery of what I was doing and what Bill was doing. The mystery of why we were doing it. The mystery of detail and attraction and friends who participated and therapists who tried to help us and the continuing, corrosive burn of not really knowing what the other was up to, was thinking, was needing. There is still so much mystery. These two scenes are the perfect distillation of all that shadowy behavior. See what that has done.

I look back on the early years of my marriage and I proceed with regret. It spirals down through me like a taproot, anchoring me to the very spot I occupy now, seven years after finding out. Had I known everything then that I know now, I wonder what would have changed. I imagine I would have married Bill anyway. I imagine he would have cheated with Susan. I imagine I would have cheated, too, because that is who I was all those years ago. It is not who I am now, and that makes the waywardness easier to acknowledge.

However, if I could change one thing without unspooling the entire history, it would be my perception of my luck in having a marriage that I should treasure. I would have strengthened that perception, tried to lock it in from the moment I met Bill at college and was drawn to him by the very mystery of attraction that I loved. Whether complete monogamy was possible for either Bill or me, I can't say. I don't know that we could have been completely true. But I wish we had been truer. So that it might have worked through to the end of our lives.

In my wallet is a photograph of Bill that still breaks my heart. It must have been taken around 1983, just after college graduation. Bill's parents were away, so of course I was visiting him at his home and we had the full run of it. Bill is lying in a rumpled bed, looking over at me. He is leaning on one tan, muscled arm, the arm of a young man, the body of a strong young man, and he is staring at me with a look of complete love. I am sure I was returning that look. I was crazy about him then. I wish I had held on to that.

That is the final mystery in every marriage, I think—the

question of where that feeling goes and why it sometimes circles back and why, for some lucky few, it never leaves. There are so many easy answers given, but none of them suffice. I think it would have been better for me to try to answer that question from the perspective of a long marriage.

But there is way too much hypothesis here. It is too much to ask of us, to undo everything in service of conjecture, of an imaginary outcome. I wouldn't know where to begin unraveling our narrative to remove the complete poisoned plotline. The first night with Tommy, maybe. When I met Declan. When I met Bill at college. On my first date. At my first dance. Who knows how far I would have to go up the river to find clear water. I just do not want regret to be the end of the story. I know a lot of marriages that are full to brimming with regret of all kinds. Why the hell is this so?

I know many marriages that bear the brunt of adultery. It seems we are a nation of cheaters, stumbling around after our own behaviors or the behaviors of the people we love. We confide in our closest friends, hide the truth from our spouses, create elaborate alibis, and commit our most profound passions to the people we are cheating with, the very people who will likely wreck our lives. Or we find out we have been deceived in the worst way. Then we fall apart, we claw at our faces and stand in the snow, bawling like cows.

The most enlightening conversations on adultery are generally held by those people committing it—in the bedroom, in the dark, between huddled friends, away from the light of useful discourse. We come to figure out that in most cases adultery answers nothing. This is obvious. Yet we do it anyway. So what it really looks like from both ends is a different and complex story. It was my story. One ordinary couple, one extraordinary set of actions, what happened, why.

People have asked me why Bill and I didn't just have an open marriage. The answer is simple. We didn't want an open marriage. If an open marriage is the route both spouses choose to go, that is one choice. It's very cosmopolitan. I know a local couple who tried this for years, and it worked to some degree. They had a lax attitude toward sleeping around. I marvel at their capacity to get past their own pasts. They had their disparate passions met through the years, and now they still have the union. There is something to be said for that. It is one choice among many.

But the idea doesn't have much appeal to me. If we were able to do it, we would all do it. I couldn't do it. Almost no one I know could do it. Hippies didn't even do well with it despite their protestations of free love and sex. They just ended up with a lot of bad, poorly conceived marriages as opposed to a lot of bad, traditionally conceived ones. However much an open marriage might have its merits, however much you think agreeing to this will be enough to clear the decks so that no one gets crushed, I find that humans are not wired this way. Not when it really counts. Lions fight off their rivals. They claw them to death. We are animals, too. Will we ever be capable of anything else? You chose this mate because you wanted to be with him or her. Meaning, him or her alone. No one else. Feeling disengaged enough to accommodate a philandering spouse is too great a price to pay for the freedoms of an open marriage. I believe in monogamy. I just haven't been very good at it.

I wonder if monogamy is possible for the species in general. Consider how young a species we are. Although the dividing line for *Homo sapiens* keeps getting moved back with each new excavation on a patch of mud in Olduvai, we are something like sixty thousand or fifty thousand years old. We are a young bunch of mammals.

There are some species that adopt mates for life. Most of them do not. Monogamy is a sophisticated take on reproduction, and I suppose it answers our neural sophistication. But how were we supposed to get this right so quickly, after only fifty thousand years?

Marriage used to be a legal term. It denoted a partnership and property and protection from the Visigoths beyond the village walls. This was apparently not good enough for us, the modern married. We wanted it to be something else. We wanted to invest it with all of our hopes and all of our conceptions of passion and romance. And now that is what we have. A freighted, overburdened, gorgeous institution that is the devil and all to get right.

In the end, I think you either cheat or you don't. It's either hardwired in you or it isn't. Infidelity may rest latent in you, but if you have that inclination, it will be difficult to resist. Or there will always be the question of it hanging, exhaustingly, in front of you. From my own perspective, I can think of only one time during my younger years when cheating was less appealing than monogamy. Right in the beginning. Right when I fell in love with Bill. Monogamy was assured then for a brief time, for something like those four days that Romeo and Juliet had. If luck and restraint had come into play, longer than that. And if it was a rare, almost unprecedented luck, for the rest of our lives. But that wasn't us. Monogamy is a question we could have asked every hour, every month, every year, during which we were trying to live as mates. I think the question would have that many answers.

There are people close to me who have never cheated, who would not consider infidelity an option now or ever. They bring me up short in my tracks, as at a wondrous new species. One girlfriend's husband has cheated on her repeatedly. I don't understand it, but she has not responded in kind. Adultery is not a choice for her. I know what I would have done. I have told her as much. That seems an easy choice. Give him a taste of it, I have said. Perhaps he will see what it feels like to be on the receiving end, and at least she would get some joy for herself in the meantime. She has not. She is one of that group of people who simply do not cheat. I know plenty of that group, too.

I wonder how they manage to avoid it. In talking with another friend, I once laid out for him an elaborate crowd of scenarios in order to gauge his conviction to monogamy. I threw down gauntlet after gauntlet. What if a woman from work asks you to drive her home and then comes on to you in the car. What if your wife says she doesn't care if you sleep with her friend (she lies). What if the most desirable woman in the world showed up naked at your home begging to have sex with you. What if your spouse would never find out. What if you stayed late, too late, with a co-worker. His answer: "I would never put myself in that situation. I have control over myself." And my response: "That's an option?!"

You see, I still gawk at monogamous people. They are a puzzlement. What is different in their makeup that they can overcome temptation is another mystery to me. But I suspect the reason they do not cheat is a subtle one. It has to do with not wanting to hurt their spouse, of course, but only partly. It only partly has to do with their vow of monogamy. In the case of those people most capable of fidelity, I think it has to do with their own honor. A sense of self that will not let them score across their own pristine slate. That's a commitment to one's self as opposed to one's spouse. Maybe that is the stronger bond after all. People who feel that from the beginning and articulate its discipline throughout their lives have a leg up on those of us who learn it later and after a huge cost.

I did not require marriage to be perfect. I did not require Bill to be perfect. I think, though, that I required romance to be perfect. I required it to last much longer than it did, and when it dimmed I required that it merely sink into a hibernation. So that occasionally it would bloom again and fulfill all its former promise. You have to walk around with your spouse on occasion and think, Yes; this is why I married you. You have to have spontaneous sex on the (carpeted) staircase. You have to watch your spouse sleeping. You have to be overcome with the joy to be had in another person, even when that person is overly familiar. It's all there. In our case we didn't tap into it, and then it was simply gone. I used to think marriage was based on passion and love. Now I see that it's based mostly on loyalty. Loyalty with warmth.

I tell my sons that I still believe in marriage, that there is no better way to go through adult life than as a married person. I believe this for anyone who wants it. But I no longer want it for myself. I had a marriage. As a legal union, it lasted eighteen years. It was enough. For a long time it gave me some of what I needed. Most important, it gave my sons a place in the world, an anchor. And it gave me them.

Marriage changes people, though. It makes us oblivious. I think it made me and Bill oblivious. The beauty of our possibility got lost in all that domestic wash. Marriage lost its glamour. It lost its big-engine purr. So I went looking elsewhere. And so did he.

It has ended up, at least for now, with my sons and me here in this little rented house outside the town proper. The front door opens almost literally into the road running in front of it. Trucks careen past and set the windows shaking. Dust rises. Cinders are thrown at the stucco and sometimes at me if I'm standing out there, timing the seizure of the mail with the passing of the next tractor trailer. Although it is the cutest little house, about two hundred years old with swayback floors and a stand-in fireplace, I did not expect to be raising my sons here.

They are at school at the moment, so all is calm. But they are divided between two homes—our rented space and the home Bill occupies with Susan—and I hate this most of all. The boys come and go too frequently, cycling clothes and suitcases and notes from teachers that we let slip through our fingers because it's tough to keep track of everything now. I have my boys for a few breathless days and then they're gone again.

This was a possibility I did not foresee when I started raising babies. That they would be gone to college and to their own lives someday, yes. That I would get to raise them only half the time, this I can't forgive. I can't forgive Bill because he promised he wouldn't force this arrangement on me. It is the worst of all the fallouts of our infidelity, that I have to share my sons out to another house.

As for Bill, I'm still trying to figure out whom I married. I don't know if I married the person I thought he was or if I married the person he was. Because he bears no resemblance now to the noble, utterly cool young man I met in college.

I realize that this kind of recognition is crucial. As long as you can locate each other, find some unmistakable trace of the person who attracted you way in the beginning, then you have a shot at a long, happy marriage. You want to feel that initial thrill as often as you can, the one that flagged your attention and desire and love and focus all those years ago so that you can continue to draw on it as you pace through the more deadening aspects of domestic life. I used to be able to recognize Bill, even after the infidelity. That is one of the reasons I wanted to keep the marriage. I still liked this man. I still loved him. It's all gone to hell now. I don't recognize Bill any longer, and my overriding feeling toward him most of the time makes me want to slink away, growling like an animal. I find that incredibly sad.

Perhaps some people think the answer of whether to cheat or not is an easy one. I am not one of them. It is a formidable choice—do you seize the chance to possibly remake the life you have now at great cost, or do you let the chance go and stay where you are? Most marriages are about comfort and stability, and boredom. Sometimes you want its polar opposite. I can't answer for everyone who asks. What do I know except the things that have happened to Bill and me and the choices we made because of them.

In grave abbreviation and by way of an answer, I can tell our story. I can say, This is what happened to us. Your path may be different. But at least know all the possibilities going in. You have to make your own choices, and then you have to inhabit them completely. Even if it means you have to pay for them completely.

In one of the few, quiet, noncombative conversations we've ever had on the subject, I asked Bill when he had fallen out of love with me. He didn't answer, though whether for courtesy or lack of self-examination I don't know. He did say that he had loved me. Then I asked him why he didn't tell me that more often. It could have gone some way in countering the mess we got ourselves into. He said, "I don't know. But I thought it every day." I realize this may sound odd to others, but it does not sound odd to me. Can you love someone and still cheat on them? If I can steal a gorgeous turn of phrase from James Joyce and Molly Bloom, Yes, I say. Yes, you can. Yes.

Most of it has turned out all right. I am still with Zane. I wrestle with what to call him, like every other adult out there who has transcended a certain age and is dating. He is my boyfriend. My partner. My mate. My *compañero*. That is the word I like best. When I say it aloud, it carries the connotation of the beloved other without the cloying overtones of cologne and hourly rates.

I am grateful for Zane's presence in my life. He was a following sea. He pushed me out of the storm and into a southern ocean. I am somewhat adrift in it, but that is easier than I thought it would be. Uncertainty is something you get used to, something you practice. And you do get better at it. For many years I thought I had a grip on my future, my life, my marriage. It had been sifting out from under me for a decade before I realized it, so my perceptions of it and of its certainty couldn't have been more baseless. It was quicksand I was standing on.

I try to remember that daily. What I think I know, I probably don't. What I think I have, I'm less likely to be sure of. This isn't necessarily a bad place to be. It feels more realistic. And that has taught me a thing or two about acceptance.

Many years ago, I remember coming downstairs one morning in January at our old house. I went out onto the back porch, which was crusty with snow. The whole of it and the lawn behind it was crisscrossed with animal tracks. The deer had been savaging the arborvitae. The trash can was overturned and a sodden mess strewn across the snow. Some beast had attacked the bird feeder, something large. And all of this had gone on while we were upstairs sleeping. We had not heard a thing. That is how I think of Bill's betrayal now. It had been going on all those years while I slept through it unaware.

So now I don't assume I know anything about what's going on outside of my own head at this exact moment in this very space. That is the only place in which my feet brush solid ground.

I have an unconventional life with Zane. Its rhythms are based on his son and my sons and their needs and the presence of ex-spouses and bills due elsewhere and homes that we do not share and responsibilities that belong only to him or only to me and social situations for which there is no clean answer. We do not share everything. It is a fractured life, even if it's a good one. My relationship with Zane would not bear the same weight that a marriage would. The new commitment, however lasting, never sits as buoyantly in the water. You have lots of ballast in the form of baggage from your past—not to mention the wisdom gained from all those mistakes—and yet it always feels as though it's more likely to capsize at the slightest gust of wind. Maybe this is just an awareness, finally, of how fragile the whole paradigm of relationship is. Of how precious it is. And how careful I need to be with it this time around, for Zane's sake and for mine.

Because I still want love. I still want to love someone. I still want to be beautiful in a man's eyes. I still want rapture. I just don't want it at any price anymore. It is easy to find someone to have sex with. It is hard to find someone to love. I still want to lie next to someone warm in bed. I just don't want the deceit and the excuses and the bedrooms in the middle of the day with someone who will become a stranger in two months. I don't want to be haunted. It was exhausting. And it amounted to almost nothing, apart from its place in memory.

Of those men I had affairs with, I have two relationships left, and those only glancingly. Tommy I haven't seen in almost twenty years. I hear things about him now and then. I heard he got married, and that he lives somewhere in central Pennsylvania, and that he drinks too much. Steven has also fallen utterly off my horizon. I tried to reach him a few years back, but it was a cautious reach across an abandoned landscape. I wanted to find out how his life is and if he is happy, but I am conscious now of the whole nest thing. Of the family nest thing. Now I don't want to be that winged creature that comes screaming in and lands in another nest and wrecks its eggs all to hell.

Terry is still a friend, although a distant one with his own life and his own family. And Declan? We send e-mails. Now and then. Not nearly enough. But there is too much to disturb in his life, too, for a friendship with history to take hold.

Whatever feeling I had for any of these men has been snuffed out by the years and by circumstance. They are as good as gone from me. Sadness crowds around this awareness. The people we love recede. The arms that wrapped around me at night or the face that hovered above me during sex or the man who waited in my driveway for a homecoming after South Carolina is now spotted, remote, and untouchable, in store aisles or driving past me on the road. I see him and I think, I know the sounds you make during sex. I know which work T-shirt looks best next to your skin. I know what you look like in the shower. I know the amount and the color of your chest hair and how often you need to shave. I know what you look like when you sleep. I know what your boots look like tossed off at the bottom of the stairs and how quickly you once ran up those stairs to catch me in embrace. This is intimate knowledge, almost sacred. And it comes in the end to not a whole lot.

Still. When I am eighty years old I will sit on my front porch, wherever that may be, and I will have sumptuous memories of these men. I will have to see if that is enough compared with the loss that infidelity has wreaked. I wonder if it will be difficult, then, to remember the desire and allure that moved me to go off and betray my husband. Tommy. Steven. Terry. Declan. They will be my weedy track back to that country.

As I age and memory piles on, I imagine it will become more difficult to distinguish the glitter from the dross. Accretion alone threatens the most fragile moments, even those that have nothing to do with infidelity—when I stood under a streetlamp in the snow with my dog Rogue, when the night sky over Sellersville glowed lavender and the buildings rose like black cardboard cutouts against it, when I woke up in my college room senior year and saw the wind luff a curtain over an open window, capturing the entire, fleeting year in one heartbreaking moment.

I remember these small harmonies with something larger than myself only because I wrote them down. Otherwise they would certainly have been lost. I would not have wanted to lose them when there are already a million others gone for good. And I would not want to lose these men entirely, either.

I will keep them, then, as my cues. While I have been assigned to move on and get old, they will stay young and beautiful in my mind. Complete eras of early adulthood attach to them. Like everything that is richly contextual, they bring it all back. I think of these men, and whole summers and geographies and emotions rise up, trailing memory. I imagine that when you are really old, remembering is what you do best. Which is good. We should have a talent to ply at every age. I will need some material to work with. I can rest assured that I have given myself plenty.

In the meantime, there is a lot to do.

Keeping order in the lives of my sons and a light hand on those reins when I am capable of it. Being with my friends. Watching my parents age out of their lives. Looking for good work. Finding a new home of our own. Loving Zane, an eccentric and self-contained man. Loving the sons I was blessed with.

The home situation is difficult for the boys and me now. Because we have moved around a lot, I have to locate their home for them in the area as opposed to one house or one street or one neighborhood. I tell them their home is all of Brandywine, the part of it that undulates in fields and valleys and forests around Kennett Square. I hope it is enough. I hope their conception of home broadens, so that it has more to do with geography than with one particular hearth. It's a stab in the dark, I know. It is even for me.

I am always driving down Beagle Road and turning the wrong way—toward our home off Brighton Road, or toward the neighborhood where we had our first house, or even toward Pineville Road where I grew up from the age of twelve. The realization that I'm not in any of those lives anymore brings me up breathless. I don't know if I just forget or if it is wishful thinking, the reflex of a desperate, pushy memory having its way with my driving habits.

In the preceding months, in real time, I have often needed some object or piece of clothing that has since been misplaced through all our moves. For instance, I cannot find my birth certificate. I can picture where it was kept in my old home. I can see it in that drawer, stuffed in among the baby books and photographs. I keep thinking, even now, that if I just hop in the car and run over to our old house off Brighton Road, I can forage through that book-case and the birth certificate will be there. As if everything we'd had still exists in some preserved form the way my mind remembers it. And I can go back whenever I need to.

I wonder what would happen if I did go back and just hung out in the yard for an hour or two. Walk the dogs around the property, go down to the stream bank with my youngest son the way we used to, read to the boys beside the tree swing, lie around in the ham-mock. There are lots of places outside that would not have changed under new owners, the way the carpet and the interior walls do. We could just breathe there for a little, accepting the charade. I wonder if it would be a restorative or if it would just emphasize our loss.

And as it turns out, the boys and I are having to move again. The rental house we live in is up for sale and we cannot afford to buy it. They have more or less accepted this second fate. They are getting better at moving. I will pack up while my sons are at school this time and have them set up in another home before dark. With any luck, no one will stumble over the crack in homes that has opened up beneath us.

I think my angel is drunk. That would explain everything. It is the best conclusion I can draw from the seven years of weird fate since the finding out in 2005 through to the present, seven years in which great sadness and great luck have been mixed like a cocktail, both shaken and stirred. And then thrown against the wall for effect.

This does not have to mean that the story ends there. What I feel now is not quite regret. It's something more useful than that. I will call it acceptance, for lack of a better term to describe the leveling calm that has settled over me. Because I cannot repudiate my life. From the perch of several years on, it still looks beautiful to me. And I don't want Bill to repudiate his life, either. What I want from him now is some real help in raising our sons. And I want having married him not to feel a burden. I want to be able to think of him with affection. It would even be good to feel a kind of familial love for him. The kind from a distance. The kind that acknowledges every failure but decides to smolder along nevertheless because we have shared a huge part of our lives.

I realize this may not make a lot of sense. But love can't be rationalized any more than it can be made into a certainty. It amazes me how much we keep expecting it to even after our marriages fail, even after the people we love bore us or drive us crazy or cheat on us or fail to move us anymore. It tempts compassion in me, how hopeless we all are. And how hopeful.

One night in October, I was out walking with my dogs in the park behind our rental house. The boys were over at their father's, and I was missing them and feeling desolate. The park was drenched in light from the full hunter's moon and a fog was coming off the ground. I could not see everything around me well, but I could hear it. Off to the right, bashing around in the weeds, there was a crowd of deer. As the dogs and I walked past, I could hear them knocking through the brush and snorting to one another as they hurried away from us. Then I heard the plosh, plosh, plosh, of lots of hooves moving through the stream. Then I heard them go up the bank on the other side and out along the flat ground where there is a lake. Then I heard all these geese lift off the lake and go shrieking into the night sky with burbled annoyance.

I laughed. Going through in my mind the triggers that had set all that motion in motion—us walking past, the deer spooking, the geese rising—I thought, I did that. I didn't intend to, but I did. Story of my life. So often the consequences I did not intend are the ones that finally push the geese into the sky. I stand here at this quiet moment and watch it all unfold, in awe.

ACKNOWLEDGMENTS

HAVE NOW TO acknowledge the people I love. But I have to do it discreetly, which is not an easy thing to do considering how much help I've received over the last few years. *Vow* itself has partly been an exercise in telling this essential story while simultaneously trying to protect people's anonymity through pseudonyms and pseudo places and pseudo names of roads. Fine with me. But what do you do for those who deserve your thanks in a big, open way?

Mercifully I can acknowledge by name my lovely editor, Kathy Belden, and my eminently cool agent, Betsy Lerner. Before I wrote a book I wondered why writers always thank the professionals first. I don't wonder anymore. Kathy and Betsy provided the kind of support most of us don't get after fifth grade, when some hawkeyed teacher pulls you out of the teeming nest and gives a name to that thing you do well. Kathy and Betsy did that for me. There is also George, Alexandra, Laura, Sara, Patti, Alexa, and Jude at Bloomsbury. Without them, I wouldn't be here.

There are editors at various newspapers who both mentored me and tolerated my newsroom antics, and for whom I am grateful. The former woman editor who dresses with wild flair, still; the male editor at the same paper who was a quiet force of guidance and fair conduct (and was also very tall); the editor who lives near me and likes art and vodka, and always has both in happy supply; the three editors who gave me a chance at the *Times*, and keep giving it. And Daniel Jones at the *New York Times*, who was so incredibly decent in the early days of this process.

The Hens—my girlfriends, the closest women in my life—are irreplaceable. We have this plan to one day buy six townhomes in an urban row and live out our old ages there, close together. (But with solid walls between. Six old women in one house? Nope.)

There are many others who should recognize themselves. The writer couple who are former neighbors, the neighbor who makes a great fire and whose house always smells like woodsmoke after October, the new parents I first befriended walking around our block, my first high school boyfriend who I ran into recently on a beach three thousand miles from home, a musician from Media, the marshmallow neighbor, some women and men whom I knew at college, the mothers of my sons' friends, various friends of my parents, my poor friend "J. D." who died too early, my beloved "Robert" and his wife, those who first read this book as a manuscript, those who like to walk the canal with me, a Philadelphia writer, a fellow reporter, and the man who kicked snow off his boots as we stood outside talking and then came back the next day for a longer visit.

My mother is proper and old-fashioned, so her support for a book about infidelity still comes as a generous surprise. Thanks and love to you both, Mom and Dad. Thanks also to my older brother and my younger sister. I could not want better siblings. My sister's generous love, which I am not always sure I deserve, continues to astonish me.

Someone mailed me an anonymous check in July of 2010, when the boys and I were moving out of our home and were worried about where we would go next. I do not know who it was but I want to express my gratitude. And thank you, Betsy, for the books.

To "Zane"—friend of my youth and man of my life—there is so much ahead of us. I am deeply lucky to have your calm, gorgeous presence in my life. And your cycling advice.

Above all, thank you to my beautiful sons, who knew about this book from the beginning and supported my writing it anyway. They are strong, smart, brave young men and clear-eyed as they come. I love you both.

A NOTE ON THE AUTHOR

WENDY PLUMP has been a newspaper and magazine reporter for over twenty years. She has written for the *New York Times*, the *Los Angeles Times* and won several New Jersey Press Association Awards. She lives in Pennsylvania with her sons. This is her first book.